Cape Horn to Port

Cape Horn to Port

Erroll Bruce

Assisted by:
Rear Admiral O. H. M. St J. Steiner, CB
Captain E. D. Norman, DSO, DSC, RN

Technical Appendix by:
Captain J. A. Hans Hamilton, RN, CEng, FIMechE, MIMarE
Captain M. A. Jones, MVO, RN, CEng., MIMechE, MIEE
Lieut. Commander R. Q. F. Evans, RN

DAVID McKAY COMPANY, INC.
NEW YORK

© 1978 Erroll Bruce
O. H. M. St. J. Steiner
D. Norman

First American edition, 1978

Library of Congress Catalog Card Number:
78-58505

ISBN: 0-679-50951-8

By the same author
Deep Sea Sailing
When the Crew Matter Most
Challenge to Poseidon
Local Knowledge
Who's Who in Yachting

Printed in Great Britain

Contents

BUCKINGHAM PALACE.

The R.N.S.A. Whitbread Round the World Race is well known to everybody interested in yachting and off-shore racing and I am sure that quite a lot of other people have heard of it. There have been two races so far with 16 entries in 1973 and 15 in 1977. This represents a wealth of experience and a mine of adventure stories. The best of these have now been put together in this book for armchair and other sailors to read as they while away the off season when they are not trying to finance the next one.

I do not think we shall ever understand why people go in for this kind of competitive sport. It is too simple to say that they just want to win. I am sure they would all like to win but I suspect that much of the reason is the sheer pleasure of taking part in an event with a lot of other people under strict rules and conditions and with the leaders setting a yardstick of performance.

Whatever the reasons for people taking part in the Round the World Race, this book makes it clear that if they went in for it for the adventure they certainly got it.

1978

Acknowledgements

This great race round the world was an epic adventure for all concerned; each yacht enacted a saga which would make a book in itself, and I hope many of these will be written. This is the story of the race as a whole, and I gratefully acknowledge information coming from so many sources.

Most of all I am grateful to Admiral 'Otto' Steiner for his valuable assistance in all aspects of this book. He led the planning, preparation and management of the race; his whole life was bound up with the competition throughout the race and he carefully noted all that went on, besides taking many photographs. It was stimulating to be with him during much of this time, so that we could continuously exchange information and opinions.

I am particularly grateful to Captain Dudley Norman, who assisted so greatly in the preparation of this book; as race secretary he was in touch with all the competitors from the time they first showed interest in entering the race, and throughout it he was constantly on duty, following every movement and ready to take instant action in case of emergencies.

Special thanks are due to Captain Hans Hamilton, Captain Mike Jones and Lieut. Commander Bob Evans for their truly valuable appendix on material and equipment. Each yacht was provided with extensive questionnaires, and these were discussed in detail with a member of this technical committee; in addition, much of the damaged equipment was scientifically examined, helped by the expertise of Bob Evans, whose official work involves investigation into air accidents. I am also grateful to Rod Stephens who provided important information from personal examination of many yachts before and after the race in which his famous firm of Sparkman and Stephens designed each of the first five yachts.

Great help came from the detailed information provided by every skipper in their official logs. In addition I particularly thank Cornelius Van Rietschoten for his help in reading some of the typescript and making helpful suggestions, besides his navigator, Gerard Dijkstra, for many vivid descriptions of life onboard *Flyer*.

Special thanks also are due to Captain Tom Woodfield for his comments on the Southern Ocean gleaned from many years experience, and particularly his personal account of *Debenhams'* adventures in the ice during the race which supplemented the stirring accounts told me by John Ridgway and his wife Marie Christine. Also special thanks to Sylvie Delinondes for writing descriptions of hazardous situations onboard *33 Export*; equally to Commander Ian Bailey-Willmot for his informative accounts from *Adventure* when she was severely tried in storm conditions. I am grateful to Philippe Hanin for the time he spent enlarging on his written accounts from *Traite de Rome*. Dr. David Dickson's letters from *Heath's Condor* were valuable in support of the accounts from Peter Blake and David Alan-Williams, besides full descriptions from Robin Knox-Johnston.

Robert James, as a very experienced yachtsman, was ever helpful in providing extra information about the thoroughly successful race of *Great Britain II*, and also of intriguing interest were the personal stories of Diana Thomas Ellam, who set out as a complete tyro in sailing.

The precision, charm and humour with which Clare Francis described some of her adventures hinted why she proved such an excellent skipper—the only one to have an unchanged crew throughout the race; also from *ADC Accutrac*, the stories told at a rattling pace on numerous occasions by Eve Bonham and 'Bumble' Ogilvy-Wedderburn, would provide material for two or three books on their own.

The log of *Kings Legend* was augmented by many personal stories, and particularly I am grateful to Bill Porter, who in this race made his third yacht rounding of Cape Horn which must surely be a record for any yachtsman.

A total of 106 men and women raced all the way round the world and I am grateful to every one of these, as all gave some information to those of us collecting information for this book. In addition 150 others competed in some part of the race, and many of these gave valuable accounts.

Thanks are due to Peter Milne for drawing the maps, and I am grateful to those who offered many thousands of photographs of the race and regret that there was not space to use more of them. Acknowledgements are made to *The Illustrated London News* for the jacket photo of the start, besides those on pages 17, 20, 21, 24; *The News*, Portsmouth page 15; Jonathan Eastland pages 42, 44, 52; Eric North pages 23, 43, 48; *Cape Times* pages 65, 67; *S.A. Yachting* page 69; *Die Burger* pages 49, 60, 61; *Auckland Star* pages 91, 99; *New Zealand Herald* pages 88, 100, 101, 102; David Alan-Williams, jacket photo of Cape Horn, pages 107, 115, 116, 118, 120, 128, 141; Skip Novak pages 113, 128, 137, 140, 149; Marie Christine Ridgway page 78; David Dickson pages 53, 54; Peter Johnson pages 36, 37; Cornelius van Rietschoten pages 81, 82, 138; Nigel Chambers page 125; Graham Carpenter page 89; Photo section H.M.S. *Vernon* page 35; Richard Creagh-Osborne pages 27, 32; Whitbread pages 12, 15, 37, 39, 41, 45, 55, 84, 85, 86, 91, 93, 94, 96, 98, 126, 131, 173, and photos by Roy Pogson for Whitbread pages 108, 143, 144, 147, 148, 150; Syndication International Ltd. pages 24, 25; Tom Woodfield page 25; Tony Dallimore page 112.

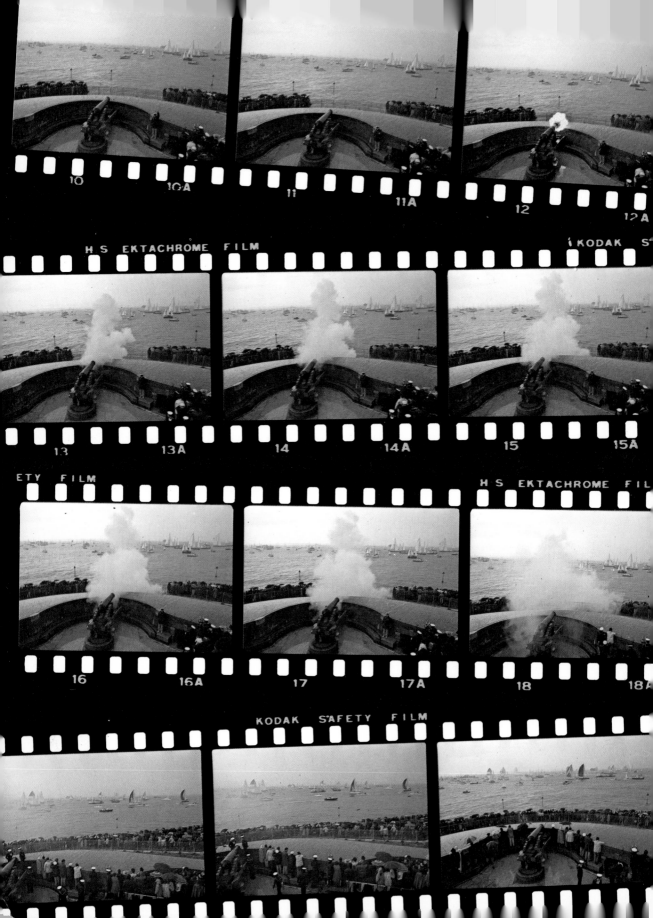

1 The Start from Portsmouth

At noon on Saturday, 27 August 1977, fifteen fine ocean yachts set out from England for a 27,000 miles race around the world, via Cape Horn. Between them they flew the national flags of Britain, France, Holland, Italy and Switzerland, besides that of the European Economic Community; they were crewed by 158 men and 10 women, including those from U.S.A., Australia, New Zealand, Ireland, Germany, Belgium and Luxembourg as well as the countries under whose flags the yachts raced.

To signal the start, an ancient cannon on Southsea Fort roared with a belch of smoke to suit the great occasion; it was fired by Ramon Carlin, the Mexican yachtsman who had won the first *Whitbread* Round the World race four years before. To support him were members of the Royal Albert Yacht Club, who handled the starting procedures at Portsmouth, and also there was the race committee of the Royal Naval Sailing Association, which had planned the race and was responsible for the whole organisation around the world.

The competitors were accompanied at the start in the East Solent by a vast fleet, including warships, ferries, pleasure launches, yachts and motor boats by the hundred, dinghies and even canoes, while many thousand spectators cheered them on their way from the fore-shores of Southsea and Portsmouth, in spite of a gloomy day with heavy rain.

A tiny canoe sheltered to leeward of the Trinity House ship *Patricia*, which was taking a day off from her duties of inspecting light-houses and lightships, for the race committee to monitor the first few initial hours of the race. 'How long will you take to reach Cape Horn in that?' shouted a wag from *Patricia*'s crew to the lone canoeist.

Small craft manned by the Royal Navy and Royal Marines patrolled a box of sea room in which the great yachts could manoeuvre for the start, but support craft which had sailed over to England from other countries were determined to give the closest support possible, so at times the racing skippers found it almost as difficult to manoeuvre inside their reserved box as outside it.

The perfect start is for the yacht to be sailing at her best speed for the conditions at the time, with her nose as close to the line as possible when the gun fires. Each competitor wants to do the same thing, but with the wind constantly varying in strength and direction, while the tidal stream also changes between one boat's length and another, such a perfect start is a stiff challenge for the quickest wits and most experienced seamen, especially when surrounded by such a spectator fleet. Should a yacht be over the imaginary line, seen by the race officer's sights, then another gun would be fired as a warning; but the over-eager yacht might have to sail on for half a mile before she found room to turn back and re-cross the starting line.

Yet on this occasion the 77 ft. long ketch *Great Britain II* was sailed with such skill that her stem seemed to be barely two feet short of the line when the gun fired. It was as though *G.B. II* was eager to show the way, as well she might; in the first *Whitbread* race four years before, Chay Blyth with his crew of para-troopers had sailed her round the world to get first back to England with sixth place on handicap; then two years later she had won the *Financial Times* race round the world. Here she was again, still owned by Chay Blyth, but skippered by Robert James, who had himself sailed in the first *Whitbread* race onboard *Second Life*, and skippered *British Steel* in the Atlantic Triangle series. His crew of 16 had each paid £4,000 to share the expenses of the venture, but some had no previous experience of sailing at all, although others were excellent sailors; yet under the guidance of Robert James, all would be experienced ocean sailors by the time they reached the Roaring Forties.

Almost level with *G.B. II* after dodging a spectator craft was the well fancied Dutch ketch *Flyer*, designed and built specially for the race. Soon after her launch in Holland she had sailed to America, then polished her racing tune by winning a race back across the Atlantic. She was skippered by her owner, Cornelius van Rietschoten, a Dutch industrialist with long experience of cruising and racing under sail. His international crew were hardened ocean racing men, many of whom had sailed her both ways across the Atlantic; the navigator was Gerard Dijkstra who had twice skippered yachts in the *Observer* Single-handed Trans-atlantic races; in the first he gave up after his yacht was dismasted, and the next time he was again dismasted, yet made repairs and still finished the course ahead of many others.

Only a few feet further back at the gun, but going so fast that she quickly took the lead, was the new varnished sloop *Heath's Condor*. The yacht was new, but her name was even newer, as two days before the start *Condor* was re-christened, when the Lloyd's insurance brokers C. E. Heath added a reputed £20,000 sponsor-ship to assist her entry. The biggest and most

expensive yacht in the fleet, with easily the tallest mast, she carried the heaviest handicap with a special factor for a particularly light mast made of carbon fibre. Her entry had been jointly prepared by two of the most experien-ced ocean sailing skippers in all the world. Robin Knox-Johnston had won the first ever sailing race round the world—the *Sunday Times* single-handed non-stop event—besides two Round Britain races; in one of these his joint skipper was Leslie Williams, who had been co-owner and skipper of *Burton Cutter* in the first *Whitbread* Round the World race, and had again teamed up with Robin for *Heath's Condor*. They were to sail and skipper in alternate legs, with Leslie Williams at the wheel when she left Portsmouth. Sailing master throughout the race was to be the New Zealand yachtsman Peter Blake, who had sailed the first *Whitbread* race in *Burton Cutter*; as the gun fired he supervised the setting of a vast spinnaker carrying a splendid great condor eagle to the design of Sir Peter Scott.

From the starter's post on Southsea Fort the next yacht to cross the line after *Heath's Condor* was the dark blue French sloop *Neptune* owned and sailed by Bernard Deguy, well known in France as a yachting journalist who had previously directed a famous sailing school. He had already raced around the world under sail, as had several of his crew.

Next came the blue French ketch *Gauloises II*, which over ten years had achieved amazing ocean racing success as the schooner-rigged *Pen Duick III*, winning a Fastnet race and two Sydney to Hobart's, under her famous owner and designer Eric Tabarly. For this race her skipper was Eric Loizeau, who became in-volved with Eric Tabarly while doing his French military service and has since then continued to gain vast experience of ocean racing. His crew had also all sailed with Eric Tabarly and include a World Champion in the 505 class, as well as several Admiral's Cup men. In the Tabarly tradition conditions for the crew were austere both on deck and below, so their

Manning the 'coffee-grinders' to trim the sheets in *Heath's Condor* needs teamwork as well as strength.

comfort had to depend upon driving a spec-
ialised racing machine really hard.

Another French yacht followed, the ketch
Japy-Hermes, built in Lymington as *Flying
Angel of Upnor* for the 1976 *Observer* Single-
handed Trans-atlantic race. She was exten-
sively refitted and modified by her owner
Patrick Therond, assisted as sponsors by the
Swiss-based Hermes group of typewriter man-
ufacturers. Her skipper, 25 years old Jimmy
Viant, raced with his father in *Grand Louis*,
which finished third overall in the first *Whit-*

bread Round the World race. Jimmy then
skippered *Grand Louis* in the Atlantic Triangle
races, finishing third overall, immediately
behind his father. His crew was partly selected
from the Marseilles College of Engineering,
whose curriculum includes research into life-
saving techniques. She was another French
yacht where creature comfort had to be
replaced by enthusiasm for hard sailing, but the
tough conditions were to be faced by Benedicte
Lunven as well as her brother Thiery.

In this group came the Swiss ketch *Disque*

15

Left: Heath's Condor off New Zealand.
Right: Great Britain II off St Catherine's
Point in the English Channel.
Below: Traite de Rome (EUR 1).
with *Debenhams* (K 1218).

D'Or, one of the production Swan 65 class of which *Sayula II* had won the first *Whitbread* Round the World race. *Disque D'Or* was skippered by Pierre Fehlmann, an electronics engineer, with a distinguished record as three times the Swiss champion in the 505 dinghy class and once runner-up in the World Championship of that class. He had also skippered an entry in the 1976 *Observer* Single-handed Trans-Atlantic race. His crew included other dinghy champions and also a member of the Swiss ice hockey team.

Then came the English ketch *Debenhams*, a production Bowman 57 class, modified for the special purposes of the race. Owner and skipper was John Ridgway, formerly a Captain in the Parachute Regiment and instructor in combat survival, who rowed across the Atlantic with Chay Blyth and then led the first expedition to follow the Amazon river from its source; he also had made the first crossing of the Grand Camp Nevada ice-cap in Patagonia, so would be accustomed to really cold conditions when they sailed among icebergs in the Southern Ocean. His crew included several instructors from the John Ridgway Adventure Training School in Scotland besides his attractive wife Marie Christine, who was used to the hardships of exploration. Then there was Alan Bose who had largely built and fitted out the yacht, besides a television team.

Another yacht to cross the line before its smoke had fully cleared, and smallest in the race, was the European Common Market blue sloop *Traite de Rome*, with her sail number EUR 1. She was previously the German Admiral's Cup racer *Pinta*, chartered for this race to the Brussels-based organisation 'Sail for Europe' to commemorate the 20th anniversary of the European Economic Community

Pierre Fehlmann, once runner up in the world 505 dinghy championship, at the wheel of the Swiss ketch *Disque D'or*.

18

The Dutch ketch *Flyer*

The British cutter *King's Legend* (K1220) and the French sloop *33 Export* (F4390).
The Swiss ketch *Disque D'Or*, green striped spinnaker, and the British ketch *ADC Accutrac*, red, white and blue spinnaker.

formed by the Treaty of Rome. Her skipper was Philippe Hanin, a 28 year old radio operator who had skippered a yacht in the 1975 Atlantic Triangle race, and also crewed in Admiral's cup races. His crew had been selected from 200 applicants hailing from all nine E.E.C. countries, and the British representative was Judith Herbert from Cornwall, who had previously sailed across the Atlantic in the crew of a French yacht.

Tenth across the starting line was the French yellow sloop *33 Export*; another of the French trio having no more than basic amenities below; like *Japy-Hermes* she was originally built for an *Observer* Single-handed Trans-atlantic race, when she was named *Raph*; she had raced in the first *Whitbread* Round the World race, finishing 12th after losing overboard one of her co-skippers, Dominique Guillet, on the second leg. Her skipper this time was 23 year old Alain Gabbay whose racing successes included a good place in the 1976 *Observer* Single-handed Trans-atlantic race sailing *Frioul 38*.

Almost level with *33 Export* came another veteran of the first *Whitbread* Round the World race. She was the blue cutter *Adventure*, one of several Nicholson 55 yachts built for the British Services Adventure Training Scheme, and, with Royal Navy crews, had finished 2nd overall in the first *Whitbread* race, actually winning three of the four legs around the world. This time skippers and crews came from the British Navy, Army and Air Force, and once again they were to change for each leg of the course so as to spread adventure training among as many Service men and women as possible. Skipper for the first leg from Portsmouth was Squadron Leader James Watts R.A.F., who learnt his sailing as a boy on the west coast of Ireland; his crew included men from each of the Services, besides Sharon Hope from the Army.

Then followed *Kings Legend*, another of the Swan 65 class, but with a single mast unlike the ketch rig of *Sayula II* which won the first race.

Owned by K.L. Enterprises, based in Jersey, she sailed under the orders of Nick Ratcliffe with Australian Hans Savimaki as skipper; there were seven Americans among her crew, besides three British which included Bill Porter, who had already sailed in two Round the World races.

Close to her at the line was another Swan 65, the British ketch *ADC Accutrac*; comfortably fitted out down below and almost certainly a ton or two heavier than *Kings Legend*, she was built in 1974 as *Pulsa*, but renamed after her sponsors, the makers of a computerised record playing turntable. *ADC Accutrac* was indeed a popular entry as her owner and skipper was Clare Francis, loved and admired by the millions who had seen her film on television taken during the 1976 *Observer* Single-handed Trans-atlantic race, when in spite of her petite appearance she had finished 13th against over a hundred powerful men, and made the best ever Atlantic crossing for a woman in 29 days.

Clare Francis had two other women in her crew. Eve Bonham had already raced with her when they won third place in the two man Round Britain Race of 1974, while 'Bumble' Ogilvy-Wedderburn from Scotland was responsible for catering. Jacques Redon, Clare's husband, was a very important member of the crew, having competed in the first *Whitbread* Round the World race onboard *Burton Cutter*, as had John Tanner, the navigator.

In the rear of the bunch came the Dutch multi-chine ketch *Tielsa*, looking a stalwart craft for the roaring forties, more than a flyer in light conditions. With her entry sponsored by the Tielsa kitchen-ware firm, she was owned and skippered by Dirk Nauta, an ex-Merchant Navy officer, who had then skippered many charter yachts, and became well known in yachting circles as skipper of *The Great Escape*,

Traite de Rome spreads her wings with spinnaker and beooper set.

which earned third place on handicap in the *Financial Times* Clipper race around the world in 1976.

The starting line had to be manned for another 20 minutes after the gun, as the Italian sloop *B & B Italia* was delayed in harbour when the pump ashore broke down while topping her up with fuel; this was essential for generating the electricity needed for radio reporting. She had a particularly intensive pre-race rush, as only two days before the start, a new mast had to be stepped, in place of one damaged on the voyage to England. First launched in 1972 as *Valentina*, she had raced offshore successfully in the Mediterranean, while her entry was sponsored by the Italian furniture company which gave her new name. Corrado di Majo was one of the youngest skippers in the race, and was only 23 when he completed the 1976 *Observer* Single-handed Trans-atlantic race.

By the time *B & B Italia* started, *Heath's Condor* was halfway to Bembridge Ledge buoy, the first and only mark of the course 'by any route seaward to Cape Town'. In the five miles to this buoy many yachts changed position as they sailed majestically through the host of spectator craft. The brilliant coloured spinnakers and other running sails made it a magnificent sight in spite of the rain and grey sky, which started to clear once they got outside the Solent.

Heath's Condor was first round the buoy, followed by *King's Legend* and *Great Britain II*, with the pack close on their sterns. Southwesterly courses were set with a quiet breeze from the north taking them down the Channel.

The rain stopped, but England was soon out of sight astern. Ahead lay the North Atlantic, South Atlantic, the Cape of Good Hope, the Roaring Forties and icebergs of the Southern Ocean; the Tasman Sea, then Cape Horn and again the Atlantic Ocean. Much else lay ahead before they would sight England again. For most it would be the adventure of a lifetime.

How came it that such a superb fleet of yachts, manned by a band of courageous men and women, were gathered for this great venture? In the next chapter we will go back to tell of this.

Above: Great Britain II in the Southern Ocean.

Centre: A good balance and a firm grip when handling a sail in *Great Britain II.*
Right: Many icebergs were met in the Southern Ocean.

2 How it All Began

The dream of a race around the world in sailing yachts must have been bandied around by almost every yachtsman who had enjoyed racing across an ocean. Certainly back in 1950, when it was quite a novelty for a 30 ft. sloop to race across the North Atlantic, I found that the most frequent subject of discussion among her crew was a sailing race right round the world, and that included Cape Horn.

Cape Horn had developed a grisly reputation as a grave yard of great sailing ships; many tried for weeks on end to beat round it against the prevailing westerly winds and current. Long winter nights, no lighthouses, icebergs and freezing spray, all made casualties numerous. Yet it seemed a reasonable challenge for a well designed modern yacht with a strong racing crew, especially if the Horn was to be rounded in the Southern Hemisphere summer, at a time when the nights are short and the temperatures moderate.

By 1950 then, two yachts cruising in their own time had successfully sailed round the world, including the Cape of Good Hope and the Horn; the first in the 1920's was an Irish cutter of 42 foot length sailed by Connor O'Brien with a crew of two or three; then in 1942 came the Argentinian Vito Dumas sailing alone in a ketch the same size, which got round the world in 13 months. In 1966 came Sir Francis Chichester and a year later Sir Alec Rose, both sailing along the route used by the wool clippers a century before. Chichester, alone in his boat, aimed to beat the speed of the

Sir Francis Chichester completes his circumnavigation in *Gypsy Moth IV*.

fully manned wool clippers, first non-stop to Australia, and then non-stop back round the Horn to England; certainly in *Gipsy Moth IV* he made astonishingly fast passages, and on the way to Sydney he sailed twice as far as any

Sir Alec Rose rounds Cape Horn in *My Lively Lady*. 1 April 1968.

yachtsman had previously sailed alone without putting into harbour. Alec Rose, in a 20-year-old cruising yacht with no pretensions to speed, also made an astonishing single-handed voyage in under a year.

Both these great voyages were like bellows to fan the growing fire of enthusiasm for a sailing race around the Horn. Thus only a year after Alec Rose got back to Portsmouth came the first race.

First Races Round the World

This was sponsored by the *Sunday Times* newspaper which offered £5,000 for the fastest non-stop single-handed voyage around the world, sailing from anywhere in Britain on any day before 31 October 1968.

Nine yachts started on different dates and from various ports, but it proved almost too great a step forward to sail alone right round the world. The attempts helped to make several well earned reputations for long distance sailing, but only one completed the course; that was Robin Knox-Johnston, who had previously sailed his ketch *Suhaili* home to England from Bombay.

Robin Knox-Johnston, a Merchant Navy man who was also a Royal Navy reservist, was a member of the Royal Naval Sailing Association, abbreviated to R.N.S.A., one of the largest yacht clubs of all, with branches spread around the world. It was inevitable that success by one of its members would find a strong echo in such a club, which had already gained a reputation for fostering ocean racing as a valuable means of adventurous training for the Royal Navy.

Rear-Admiral 'Otto' Steiner, a very experienced yachtsman who was then the R.N.S.A. flag officer responsible for ocean racing, quickly appreciated that a race round

The Mexican yacht *Sayula* off Cape Horn on her way to win the first fully manned yacht race round the world.

the world with fully crewed yachts would catch the imagination of the Association's members as the ultimate in adventurous sailing, and he soon found that the Royal Navy officially was closely in sympathy with the idea. He was invited to go ahead, seeking financial backing, as such an event was clearly beyond the Association's financial resources.

He decided to form a race committee of people who had raced or cruised over long distance, with a working knowledge of the seas, weather and racing problems that would be encountered right round the world, and also with experience of race management. The first who agreed to serve was Sir Alec Rose, who had been a member of the Association for several years. Some very experienced members of the Association were likely competitors in any such race, while others would be prevented by seagoing naval duties from working consistently on such honorary functions over a period of two years and more.

Robin Knox-Johnston was an obvious choice, but his professional duties and vigorous participation in ocean racing meant that he could serve as an adviser, and not take on the regular functions of a race committee member. Sir Francis Chichester, although not an R.N.S.A. member, also agreed to serve as adviser, as did several senior naval officers with special technical knowledge of matters such as radio communications and meteorology.

All this led to the undoubted success of the first *Whitbread* Round the World race; 14 yachts from six different countries completed the course, and in the race to the finish ten yachts got back to Portsmouth within a week of each other, while on handicap a mere 11 days covered the first six yachts over the entire 27,000 miles.

New Race Announced

Soon after the finish, the R.N.S.A. decided that there was likely to be a demand for another race round the world to start in four years time. The first essential for a new race was sponsorship, as you cannot run a world-wide organisation on a dime even if its 'directors', and so many other helpers, give their services for nothing. There was no doubt in the minds of the planning committee that *Whitbread*, the famous brewing firm, should be invited to sponsor the second race, after establishing such excellent relationships with the R.N.S.A. in the first, and this was agreed by the Board of Whitbreads. Thus, when His Royal Highness The Duke of Edinburgh presented the prizes for the first race in London's Mansion House, he also announced the new race.

However, between these two *Whitbread* events, a new race was sponsored by the *Financial Times* newspaper, with the technical supervision of the Royal Ocean Racing Club. Called the Clipper Race, it stopped only in Australia, like the wool clippers of old.

Such a lengthy sail, with just one stop in harbour and the prize going to the fastest time, irrespective of size and rig, had a more limited appeal to amateur yachtsmen. Only four yachts started from London, and on the leg round the Horn the leader had to compete mainly against the voyage of a record-holding clipper more than a century before, as her contemporaries were spread out too far astern to give her a race.

Rear Admiral 'Otto' Steiner, chairman of the race committee.

Race Committee and Advisers

Some felt that this small entry showed that the demand for such very long races had been satisfied for many years to come. Yet Admiral Steiner, by then Commodore of the R.N.S.A., felt that a second race on the Association's lines, started four years after the first, would attract about the same entry again. The two essential differences from the Clipper race were, first, that handicaps allowed a wide range of yachts a reasonable chance of winning, and then that three stopovers instead of one gave increased interest to crews. In setting up and running the first race Admiral Steiner had travelled twice round the world and gone onboard every yacht as she finished each leg, so had close knowledge of the point of view of competitors, besides exceptional experience of the organisational problems; he was invited to take on chairmanship of the race committee again and although this was an extremely demanding honorary task, he agreed to do so yet again.

The rest of the first race committee had joined their chairman in asking that new blood should take on for the next, if possible making use of those who had already sailed in the race round the world. Indeed, Chief Petty Officer Mike Bird, a mate in the crew of *Adventure* for the first race, agreed to serve and his naval duties in Her Majesty's Yacht *Britannia* kept him in touch with many parts of the world, although he could not always attend regular organising sessions. Commander Patrick Bryans R.N., a skipper of *Adventure* in the first race, also joined the committee but was soon afterwards appointed to duties in the U.S.A., and other former competitors found that their naval duties prevented such honorary work; so some of the first committee were drafted for service again; thus Captain Hans Hamilton R.N., who had also been a member of the Clipper Race committee, was once more Vice-Chairman, while Sir Alec Rose was essential as an 'elder statesman' of adventurous sailing. Captain Dudley Norman R.N. brought administrative continuity by remaining as the professional race secretary.

'Surely you can find someone younger', the author of this book protested to Otto Steiner when requested to continue serving for a second race. 'Well, Erroll, you must have learnt

The race committee in session on board Peter Richardson's yacht. Left to right: John Fox, Mike Bird, Mike Jones, Alec Rose, Hans Hamilton, 'Otto' Steiner, Dudley Norman, Erroll Bruce, Reggie Hughes, Peter Richardson.

something from racing four times across the Atlantic and sailing in a handful of Admiral's Cup teams', answered the Admiral. 'The thing is we need you.'

From *Whitbread*'s agreement to sponsor this sporting event of worldwide importance, it followed that John Fox, by then their promotion director, should once again serve on the race committee. A newcomer to the committee was Reggie Hughes, retired from the Corps of Naval Constructors, who was to take charge of the Race Control Organisation, which, with the help of a big team of volunteers, plots the positions of all competing yachts throughout the race and answers any immediate questions from the Press day and night. Another newcomer was Captain Mike Jones R.N., who had been Rear Commodore (Offshore) of the R.N.S.A., and previously Sailing Master of the Royal Yacht *Bloodhound*; yet another was Commander Peter Richardson R.N., whose

experience as Assistant Queen's Harbour Master at Portsmouth was important, considering that a fleet of many hundred spectator craft were expected at the start. Finally, as ex-officio member representing the Ministry of Defence, was Commander Laughton R.N., of the Directorate of Public Relations.

This made up a race committee of ten, which was none too many as for all it was honorary service, and experience had shown that at least three needed to be present for several weeks at each stopover, to assist the committees formed from experienced yachtsmen living in these places.

Then came the special advisers. Captain M. C. Henry R.N. was the link with the Naval Staff as its director of Naval Operations and Trade. Another adviser turned into a competitor himself; this was Captain Tom Woodfield, an Elder Brother of Trinity House who after 20 years in the Antarctic aboard survey ships, must have known as much about the Southern Ocean as any man alive. Having offered his advice to all competitors, he then boarded one of them in Cape Town and showed the way to Antarctic waters.

Long before this final team was completed, the planning nucleus had set up the course and made the preliminary moves. We had the experience of the first *Whitbread* race to build on, but were free to make any changes; meantime this small committee was keeping its hand in by organising the final leg, from Rio de Janeiro, of the Atlantic Triangle, which started with a French organised leg to Cape Town and then a South African organised leg to Rio.

Multihulls

Part of the R.N.S.A.'s interest in this race came from the hope that it might give us experience of long distance multihull racing. Some members had been keen to sail multihulls

Nigel Tetley's *Victress*, flying the RNSA burgee, was the first multihull to sail round the Horn, and made the first trimaran circumnavigation.

in the first *Whitbread*, but this had been restricted for a variety of reasons. One was that we had quite enough problems planning a long race for monohull yachts ranging in length from about 50 to 80 feet overall, whose performance we could hope to predict. We had not enough information to predict similar performances of fully crewed and well laden multihulls.

However a special multihull race to Rio would give valuable information, which would be greatly augmented if these multihulls then joined with the monohulls for the 5,500 mile race back to Portsmouth.

To help with this we were joined by Mike McMullen, author of the classic book *Multi-hull Seamanship* and one of the most experienced trimaran long distance racing men in all the world, who had also raced across the Atlantic in a monohull. The *Whitbread* Multihull race was planned in detail, a course criss-crossing the Atlantic Ocean, with stops in the Azores, Florida, Freetown and Barbados.

Sadly enough none of the potential starters had in time passed the stringent pre-race requirements imposed for the safety of competitors, so this first attempt at a long distance fully manned multihull race came to nought. Sadder still, Mike McMullen was himself lost at sea in his trimaran the following year. Yet he, and Lieut. Commander Bob Evans R.N. who succeeded him as our multihull adviser, gained committee agreement that multihulls, although not eligible for the handicap awards as there was no means of assessing their handicaps, should be allowed to join the race round the world if they complied fully with the rigid safety requirements of the race.

Safety Requirements

The safety rules that evolved for the race round the world were undoubtedly rigid and it soon became clear that they inevitably required so much weight onboard that only a very large multihull could comply without losing most of her design advantages.

The approach to safety at sea by the racing committee was undoubtedly influenced by the fact that the sea was our profession. We felt that any rules and regulations should be for the benefit of the seafarer and not merely 'yard-arm clearers' for higher authorities and organisers; also they should be capable of enforcement. Yet we were convinced that above all the safety of a vessel at sea must remain the responsibility of the skipper. Though he may act on advice from others—and would be foolish not to listen to advice—the man in charge must make the decision; whether he should reduce speed or canvas; whether the course he is taking is prudent; whether he is over-driving his ship or his crew. A good skipper draws on his experience and that of others; he takes advice and obeys mandatory rules, such as the rule of the road.

The course led through vast stretches of the Southern Ocean where ships would seldom be seen, so life rafts were required to a much higher specification than would be acceptable for normal races.

The skipper's responsibility for safety needs to be supported by certain essential requirements ordained for the type of race.

There is always an element of risk when facing the winds and the seas, but there is a great difference between calculated risk with planned resources, and a foolhardy gamble without proper equipment. The Offshore Racing Council lays down the minimum safety standards for yachts, but these are the minimum, allowing that many offshore races are in relatively safe waters, with help not too far away.

Trans-ocean racing changes all that. The land quickly disappears over the horizon and with it the comfort of search and rescue organisations. Furthermore yachts do not necessarily keep to shipping lanes and, in the race round the world via the Horn, they cross great stretches of ocean where shipping is rarely seen.

Accurate and regular position reporting is essential and mandatory in the interest of yachts and crew safety, so failure to report without valid reason carries penalties. Inter-yacht communication periods were established mainly for safety purposes—and for the comfort it engenders to know that one can talk to someone else, or pass one's position via a yacht in a better position to do so. You can feel very lonely in the Southern Ocean if your radio breaks down.

An ample crew to deal with any problem over several weeks is a vital safety precaution, especially as individuals can be disabled or even lost overboard. Thus five crew is set as the minimum for such racing.

Very small yachts can cruise safely, but for safe racing in the Roaring Forties the size is restricted to International Offshore Rating Class I yachts, as if smaller yachts comply with all the international requirements, besides our own special requirements, they will scarcely be able to race fully crewed over the distances involved. Their participation could entail more stops—and this in itself poses problems in the Southern Oceans—with greatly increased elapsed times which in their turn would bring new problems of timing and greatly lengthening the overall time for the race. Safety harness for each member of the crew is a normal offshore requirement but this race also demands permanently rigged life-lines to which it can be clipped for moving about on deck. Then we added to the Offshore Racing Council's requirement for an emergency life-raft capable of carrying the yacht's crew; we required two life-rafts and also that each should have inflatable double bottoms as protection against hypothermia in the Southern Ocean.

Thus detailed special regulations for the race had to be drawn up and published in ample time for any potential competitor to adapt his yacht and provide the equipment; this should be done some two years before the start, and the first details were published at a Press conference in London during May 1975.

Race Rules

Owners also had to know the general rules for which their yachts would need to be prepared, and here lay a difficult problem. We were anxious to race as far as possible under the various international codes, but the racing rules of the International Yacht Racing Union, besides the International Offshore Rule for measurement of rating, were liable to change each year. Those entering for the *Whitbread* Round the World race, which might take two years to prepare and eight months to sail, could find that some new regulation, perhaps even passed when the race was in progress, rendered the yacht ineligible.

It was decided that although the final leg of the race would be in 1978, the international regulations in force in 1977 would decide eligibility, so long as any yacht on starting or joining the race had a valid rating certificate, but the I.Y.R.U. gave exemption for this race from its 1977 rule which forbids a yacht's name that could be held to promote a firm or product.

Sponsorship

Sponsorship was an essential requirement for such a race, as exceptionally few private individuals could be expected to undertake the heavy cost involved in campaigning a yacht, just as it would be impracticable for any yacht club to mount such a major event without support such as was given by the firm of Whitbread, whose chairman Alex Bennett wrote of sponsorship:

'In medieval times patronage stemmed solely from the monarchy and the very rich nobility. In the 18th and 19th centuries, explorers and creative people often owed much of their success to the material aid they received from various private philanthropists. Today, though, all has changed. In place of the wealthy patron of earlier ages, the duty now rests with business companies and other large organisations which, in the main, are the only non-governmental bodies that still have the resources to undertake effective sponsorship. A duty, yes, but with tangible results—for the participants, spectators and the public at large—because many present-day sponsorships have led directly to such practical benefits as safety improvements on the roads or at sea, improvements in international relations, and the raising of standards generally in cultural, sporting and other spheres of human activity.'

Dealing with the particular race he continued:

'We feel that the spectacle of the friendly competitive spirit, between some of the world's finest sailors, will help to forge new bonds of mutual interest and understanding between people of a great many different nationalities— and not only those whose first love is sailing. The race will unite vast numbers of people: the designers, architects and builders of the yachts; the race organizers, here and abroad; and, perhaps most important of all, the spectators around the world who will be avidly following the progress of crews and yachts.'

Entries Come In

It was in January 1976 that the first to become an actual competitor came forward with definite plans for entry; this was Clare Francis, the yachtswoman who had sailed so well in the Single-handed Trans-atlantic race. Soon after that Leslie Williams and John Ridgway made their intentions clear, while a veritable flood of enquiries came from France, with a firm request from Pierre Fehlmann in Switzerland, another from Dirk Nauta in Holland and yet another from Philippe Hanin in Brussels.

By the beginning of 1977 the Race Committee had begun to feel that their efforts should turn more to a high standard of entries rather than numbers. With a view to the facilities available at the start and at stopovers, it was agreed that only really suitable entries should be encouraged, and that we would prefer 15 to 20 top class yachts of genuine ocean racing ability to a larger fleet which included several whose age or design would probably mean that they were soon far behind the main fleet.

Indeed 15 was the number that finally completed their entry formalities, and gathered at Portsmouth for a full week of scrutiny, briefing and social activities. It then became clear that the hopes for a top quality fleet were fully realised.

Yachts Gather at Portsmouth

The creek in H.M.S. *Vernon*, a naval training establishment just inside the entrance to Portsmouth harbour, became the centre of a unique gathering, not only of fine ocean yachts but also a group of men and women who quickly started to develop into an extraordinary community, which became more and more closely knit as they faced common dangers, hardships, joys and pleasure on their voyage around the world.

It was an intensely busy scene around the creek. Prominent was a vast caravan where a medical team from the British United Pro-

The creek in H.M.S. *Vernon* was the centre for the competing yachts.

Captain Mike O'Kelly welcomes to his quarter deck the famous Whitbread greys bringing beer to the yachts. Charles Tidbury (left) and Raymond Seymour make the introduction.

vident Association offered free health checks, with medical supplies and advice before the start, and the promise of more at the stop-overs; then many of the firms sponsoring yachts had brightly set up stands to show their interest. Captain Michael O'Kelly R.N. on his -quarter-deck', sanctum of naval customs and tradition, met the *Whitbread* grey horses pulling a dray which brought supplies of beer for the yachts; these famous horses were quite at home on big occasions with large crowds, and one felt they would be far too diplomatic to leave an offering of manure in such a place.

The public were invited and swarmed in, taking a lively interest and sometimes tripping over the electric leads of the T.V. men, who vied with a whole host of pressmen for the best stories. Lieutenant Commander Roger Harris R.N., in charge of the creek, was firmly polite in sending to other moorings the numerous support craft that was gathered in Portsmouth, so that competitors would be unscathed by bad weather such as the gale which blew up one night; also they needed freedom to move off elsewhere for final slipping, replacing a mast, refuelling or making good some defects disclosed by the team of scrutineers.

Scrutineers

The scrutineers, under the lead of Commander David Bird R.N., had a responsible task to complete. Each skipper was first given a full check list, and when that was ready, the scrutineer would go through it item by item, noting any item missing or defective; only when these were rectified would a clearance be authorised and a signed form passed to the Race Office. In practice the close attention to detail demanded by the scrutineers was welcome; safety and emergency equipment which might have been buried underneath a mountain of stores was brought to light and properly stowed. Each crew had the satisfaction of knowing that nothing had been forgotten or overlooked.

Next, crews lists, with addresses, passport numbers and individual photos were required to ensure that Race Control knew who was onboard each yacht; only when these were complete, besides the scrutineer's form, were yachts clear to start.

Hospitality

As each yacht arrived she had been boarded by her particular volunteer liaison officer, male or female, who handed out mail and was available to give advice on local affairs and facilities. Each was also adopted by a different local pub in the Portsmouth area. On the first evening, when the visitors were 'on the house', they met the pub's regulars and were introduced to the peculiarly English community of the 'local'.

Then there were parties; some were formal, such as the reception by the Lord Mayor of Portsmouth at the Guildhall, or the R.N.S.A.'s official welcome to all crews held in H.M.S.

Stores and provisions laid out on the pontoon in H.M.S. *Vernon*'s creek, ready for the crew of *B and B Italia* to embark them.

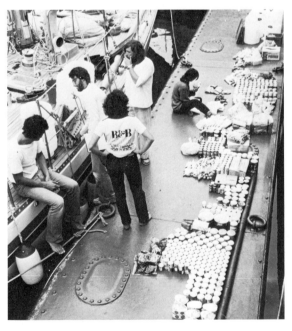

It was a busy time for all in H.M.S. *Vernon*'s creek, and there were normally numerous supporters and onlookers, but the crew of *Japy-Hermes* (left) were soon ready to go.

Vernon, and some were less so. On the eve of departure, the Directors of Whitbread gave a magnificent farewell party in H.M.S. *Dolphin*, the Navy's submarine base at Gosport.

When morning came on Saturday, 27 August, the strong wind of the previous day had eased, but it was a grey day with rain not far away. Everyone onboard the yachts seemed keen to get on with the race, and they could look forward to ample sunshine once they had sailed out of the channel and across the Bay of Biscay.

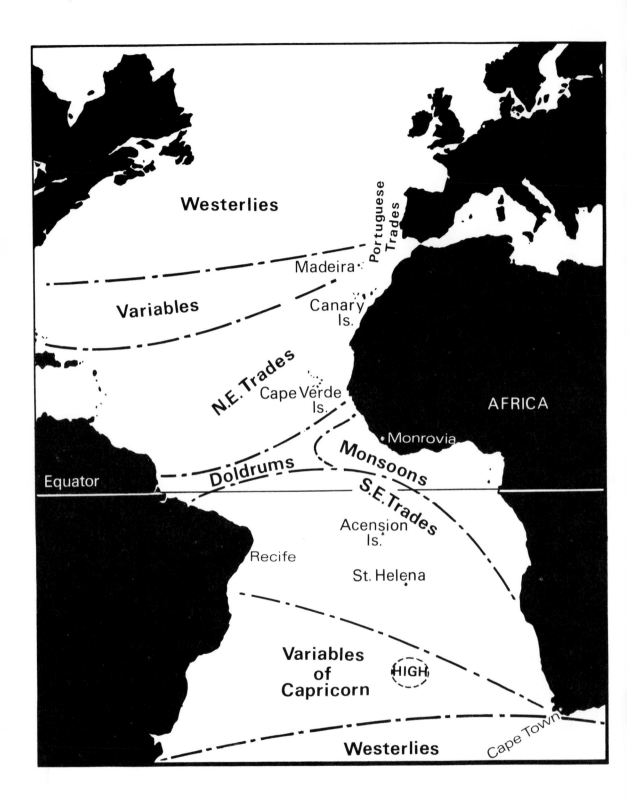

Westerlies

Portuguese Trades

Variables

Madeira

Canary Is.

N.E. Trades

Cape Verde Is.

AFRICA

Monrovia

Equator

Doldrums

Monsoons

S.E. Trades

Acension Is.

Recife

St. Helena

Variables of Capricorn

HIGH

Westerlies

Cape Town

3 Bay of Biscay to Cape Verde

Sailing out of the English Channel and across the Bay of Biscay, the course is through the Westerlies of the North Atlantic, although in practice winds may blow from any direction in September with a preponderence from westerly sectors. From Cape Finisterre onwards, the 'Portuguese Trades' in September normally blow from a northerly direction all the way to the Canaries. Past the Canary Islands comes a wide belt of the north-east trade winds, which blow with a remarkable constancy, usually accompanied by pleasant weather with ample sunshine, occasional rain and distinctive trade wind clouds of fleecy broken cumulus.

Then come the doldrums, which in September are normally first met some ten degrees, or 600 miles, north of the equator. This is a belt of clammy hot atmosphere, with frequent thunderstorms, bringing heavy rain and strong squalls, scattered amongst the region of very light variable winds. This doldrum belt across the Atlantic is usually two or three hundred miles wide, tending to be narrowest towards the South America side. In July the south-west monsoon of the Gulf of Guinea stretches out nearly halfway across the ocean from Africa below the doldrums, but by late September it is retreating towards the African coast, so the course to the west can go straight from the doldrums to the south-east trades. This brings back the pleasant trade wind weather; in September they are normally much stronger than the north-east trades, but on a course for

Cape Town they are right on the nose. They will probably be carried until down to within a few hundred miles short of the latitude of Cape Town.

Then comes the real tactical puzzle with the Variables of Capricorn. In them there is a great area of high pressure, known as the South Atlantic High, wandering around between South Africa and South America, carrying in its centre light winds which may well be a more testing barrier to sailing craft than the doldrums.

When the fleet set out from the coast of England the yachts were sailing through quiet seas with a gentle northerly breeze which carried them quickly down the English Channel. Under a vast expanse of sail *Heath's Condor* was plotted from the radar of *Patricia*, the Trinity House ship, as sailing at 11 knots in the lead; but all were making excellent progress in proportion to their size.

Strong westerly winds, perhaps up to gale force, are not unusual in these waters at that time of year. So perhaps they were fortunate; at least the less experienced crews must have welcomed the opportunity to get their sea legs in such easy conditions. Yet a group of the well tested crew of *Flyer* had been heard before the start to pray for a good westerly gale, so as to give full benefit to their practice runs twice across the Atlantic compared with those who were less well prepared.

In the evening the wind freshened to make steering more difficult, with the yachts surfing at times. It is a thrilling experience to be at the wheel of a big yacht with every sail full as she rides the top of a wave, reaching speeds far above her normal maximum. The wave top rises up in a swirling torrent either side of the cockpit, the wheel becomes stiff with the extra pressure on the rudder; if she starts the ride pointing wrong it may be too late to prevent her swinging round in a broach, heeling over until the spinnaker and main boom are dragging through the water. When struggling at the wheel, especially in the dark, if often feels as

though the wild ride goes on for ages, yet an unemotional stop watch would show that it had actually been a matter of seconds.

Even the best of crews were kept busy that first night. *Heath's Condor* blew out her medium spinnaker just before midnight, while in *ADC Accutrac* two spinnakers had been blown out by then; one was a very light tri-radial sail of only 1.5 oz. material, and she seemed unlucky to lose it before dark, when the wind was still quite light; yet it was blowing a good deal harder when her 2.2 oz. radial-head spinnaker followed a couple of hours later. All this would mean much work in sewing up the torn sails, and fortunate indeed were the yachts which had experienced sailmakers and good sewing machines onboard.

With her Atlantic race behind her *Flyer* quickly got into the rhythm of long distance racing. Her crew was organised in two watches of five men, with the skipper and cook out of watch but available to back up if needed. By day, each watch was on deck for six hours, one from 8 a.m. until 2 p.m., and then the other taking on until 8 p.m. Then came three night watches of 4 hours, with each group getting the 'dead man's watch', from midnight until 4 a.m., on alternate nights.

On this first night *Flyer* went particularly well, keeping her sails well under control and steadily overtaking *Kings Legend* in the middle watch. Yet soon after the other watch took over at 4 a.m., the helmsman needed to be thoroughly alert as a cruising yacht, with no navigation lights showing at all, was suddenly sighted very close ahead. Only quick reaction at that rather sleepy time before dawn prevented a collision.

There was a good number of ships around that first night, and even when carrying the correct navigation lights, rain showers meant that they were not always seen until fairly close.

(Opposite) Some of the well tested crew of *Flyer* prayed for a good gale at the start.

With daylight next morning the wind became light, yet less than 24 hours after the start *Heath's Condor* was leading round Ushant into the Bay of Biscay.

G.B. II, just in sight astern, decided to sail inside Ushant; strong tides make it a tricky passage among rocks and reefs if visibility should be poor, but an interesting short cut for a skipper who knows the waters well.

The yachts which did not catch the tide at Ushant just about stood still until the tide again turned in their favour, and by then the wind had fallen away to nothing; when the first zephyrs came again, they were from the west.

This relief from the bumpy seas of the night before was welcomed by at least some of the crew in *Heath's Condor*, as apart from the torn spinnaker to be sewn up, there were endless jobs of stowing gear below which required their watch routine to be amended until all was shipshape. 'Jobs remaining seem endless', recorded Leslie Williams, her skipper.

For Clare Francis in *ADC Accutrac*, following her expensive first day with two spinnakers in need of repair, the next day produced some surprises; first of all the Sunday morning church service was interrupted by the surprise invasion of a bat, and then at midday the main aerial cascaded onto the deck after parting at the masthead. However, contact had just been made via Brest radio for the first of Clare Francis' broadcasts for Capital Radio and someone onboard suggested that the shattered aerial was due to some male chauvinist listener in London abhorring the idea of a woman captain. These regular broadcasts from the yacht became increasingly popular among the listeners in London, for whom the adventures aboard a yacht actually competing in the race were brought home vividly. Most of them must have appreciated the qualities needed by a young woman to organise her entry and sail her yacht, but listening to her they must surely have felt how marvellous it would be to show the same courage, personality and skill themselves.

Once in the Bay of biscay, few seemed

Gerard Dijkstra, navigator of *Flyer* takes a sun sight with his sextant.

content with the weather as they tacked into light headwinds, making slow progress. However *Flyer*'s navigator Gerard Dijkstra was able to log of a middle watch 'Beautiful night, full moon'. Later that day they sighted four whales close to the yacht, and one dived right under it. Any of the competing yachts could be seriously damaged, or even sunk, by collision with a large whale, so they are watched carefully when nearby. Indeed, the Italian yacht *Guia*, competing in a Royal Naval Sailing Association race from Rio to Portsmouth two years before, had been sunk by a whale; reports of smaller yachts sunk by whales are not infrequent, while sometimes crews felt that their craft was deliberately attacked. Sir Peter Scott, the famous naturalist, wrote that after discussing this with marine biologists he could not find enough clear evidence to suggest a reason for such attacks. He advised that those in small craft who feel threatened by whales should start an engine or bang on the hull, as

Sharon Hope at the wheel of *Adventure* in fresh conditions with the yacht hard on the wind.

the 24 hours to noon on 1st September; *Traite de Rome* managed only 72 miles, while *G.B. II* covered only one mile further; but it must have been consolation to several of those onboard her with no previous experience of deep sea sailing that they had crossed the Bay of Biscay without feeling seasick; they would have been delighted, had they known it at that stage, that no one onboard was to be seasick throughout the whole 40 days of the voyage to Cape Town.

Heath's Condor, scarcely ahead but further out to sea, made good a paltry 35 miles that day. Her log at midnight recorded 'Wind Nil' followed by the comment 'Flip Flop power rules. What a waste of effort'. Actually the flip flop action of a sail, with no wind to steady it, can be as damaging as the strains of strong winds. The previous afternoon she ripped a panel out of the floater when it snagged on the staysail halyard block in a roll.

The real pleasure of a calm at sea comes when it stops, with the first breath of moving air that follows it. The mirror surface of the sea is gently ruffled by catspaws which saunter away and then disappear. Soon the wind fills in to a firm pattern of low waves; these steadily grow as the wind speed increases to some ten knots, or nautical miles an hour. With any further increase an odd white horse is seen, as some of the energy from the wind is dissipated by the wave breaking.

By then the lightest sails have been replaced by those of heavier material. In such calm conditions it is a matter of seconds only for the watch on deck to lower the drifter and hoist a light genoa in its place. The next change, perhaps to a medium genoa, will take a bit longer as the sail is heavier to handle and by then the deck will be less steady. When later it comes to changing the heaviest sails, it can be an exhausting struggle, fighting against the power of the wind, sweating in thick oilskins on a heaving deck as the spray hurtles over.

So the wind came to them, and generally it was from the northerly sector, allowing spinnakers, tall boys, mizzen spinnakers, and

such mechanical noises might warn a whale that the boat is not another animal, which could be a rival or a source of food.

Light conditions continued on and off across the Bay of Biscay. As *Adventure* approached Cape Finisterre under floater and drifter her mate, Red Searle, reported that in the search for wind she went in to within a cable of the rocks—that means 200 yards, which is close enough to a strange coast, even on the quietest night, and just before midnight she gybed to clear Cape Torinana. *Traite de Rome* remained in close company with her, but before dark two other yachts were seen astern edging out to seawards. One of these was *B & B Italia*, and the other was *G.B. II*, which that day sighted not only each of those competitors but also *Disque D'Or* and *33 Export*.

For several yachts that proved the slowest day on all the course to Cape Town, slower even than in the notorious calms of the doldrums. For instance *Adventure* logged only 80 miles for

whatever else would drive their yachts south-wards past Spain and Portugal.

Three days after her worst run on the leg to Cape Town *Flyer* made a satisfying run of 231 miles in 24 hours, tacking down wind to keep the wind 30 degrees on the quarter. A sailing craft can generally run faster with the wind on the quarter than right astern, and with a keen crew it may pay off to sail the extra distance this involves.

Swiss *Disque D'Or* was at one stage that day only three miles from *Flyer*, but when she gybed, her red spinnaker with two white bands soon disappeared and her gybe must have been at just the right moment, as she was next reported ahead of *Flyer*.

Meantime *Heath's Condor* was having radio problems; this was an important racing matter, as the race rules required that yachts should report their positions twice a week, both for their own safety and also so that those nearest could be directed to stand by any other yacht in trouble. Leslie Williams onboard *Heath's Condor*, using short range VHF through a

Spanish station, was able to get a message through to Robin Knox-Johnston, in England, that his main radio receiver was ineffective. This was passed on to the Race Control at Portsmouth which sent a radio message to *G.B. II*, then the nearest yacht, asking her to make contact with *Heath's Condor* on the inter-yacht net.

Nothing was heard by *Heath's Condor*, but while her crew struggled with the radio tuning, which seemed to be affected by the dimmer light control, a dove landed onboard.

'Ingenious chap, Robin,' suggested one of the crew, 'he's set up a pigeon post already.' But unfortunately the bird could no more be tuned to the needs of race communications than could the long range radio.

Again using VHF through Radio Coruna, Leslie Williams was able to speak with Robin Knox-Johnston, and asked that a spare radio set be flown to Tenerife.

Arrangements were quickly made to fly out the set, but now well away from the Spanish coast, it proved much more difficult to let the

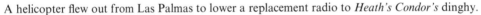

A helicopter flew out from Las Palmas to lower a replacement radio to *Heath's Condor's* dinghy.

yacht know where it could be picked up, although nearly all the yachts were asked to try and get through to her that it was being flown out to Las Palmas. Leslie Williams decided to steer a course between Tenerife and Gran Canaria, hoping to get further information on short range VHF when close to the Canaries. He had an anxious wait, as a lighthouse on Tenerife had already been sighted when radio contact was successful at last. News came that the spare radio set was in Las Palmas, not Tenerife; however Lloyd's agent agreed to arrange a helicopter rendezvous between the two islands.

Greatly relieved by this information the crew of *Heath's Condor* enjoyed a fantastic moon-light sail past the lights of Santa Cruz. With the dawn came the dramatic arrival of a helicopter. A helicopter's lifting hook caught in a yacht's rigging as she rolled could be a death trap, so a dinghy was trailed astern, manned by Jack Kehoe and Justin Smart; they quickly took delivery of the precious radio receiver, which was soon in action.

Robert James, skipper of *G.B.II*.

About this time another yacht made use of the rule allowing gear to be picked up at any port en route. From French *33 Export* part of a rigging screw on the forestay had been dropped overboard, and it was found that there was no spare one onboard. She sailed to Madeira, picked up the spare part in Funchal, and sailed on her way again without any penalty beyond the time spent in diverting from her course. This proved quite expensive as from then on *33 Export* seemed to get on the wrong side of the weather systems.

While *Heath's Condor* was picking up her radio set off Tenerife, *G.B. II* sighted the island 12 miles ahead. Things had settled down extremely well onboard, and her crew were able to watch with special interest her progress compared with the positions day by day when four years before the yacht had raced over the same leg to Cape Town skippered by Chay Blyth. This time Chay's wife, Maureen, was able to speak by radio direct to Robert James, the skipper this time; on 7 September she told him that his own wife, Naomi, was setting out that day from Dartmouth for her sail around the world, single-handed onboard the yacht *Express Crusader*.

Most of the fleet sailed through the Canary Islands, but *Japy-Hermes* took a more westerly course; her log recorded the positions she estimated for most of her rivals, helped by the nightly inter-yacht radio chat, popularly known among the crews as 'Children's Hour'. This was looked forward to eagerly by most crews but *Heath's Condor* did not join in as she had a good many other matters to attend to, while *Neptune* preferred to keep her position to those who might sight her. Actually she was not far away from *Japy-Hermes* as they both passed outside the Canaries, and were already set on a track well to the westward of the others.

The problem of a course through the Canaries was to avoid being becalmed in the wind shadow of the high land. Thus *Adventure* passed at fine speed between Palma and Gomera Islands, but then the wind became

ADC Accutrac.

light and variable in the lee of Tenerife. This extended for 60 miles from its 12,000 foot high mountain, and to cover that took 18 hours, 22 sail changes, and two spinnaker wraps, which each entailed a man going aloft. Her rivals which passed to the east or the west had no such troubles, so she was unlucky that the decision to sail through the islands, instead of outside them as originally planned, may have cost her a precious eight hours. *ADC Accutrac* had steered between the same islands the day before, and covered over 200 miles in the 24 hours from the time when Palma was abeam; indeed, in the first few hours the wind freshened to blow out her worker spinnaker, which had to be replaced for a time by the storm spinnaker.

Past the Canaries all picked up the north-east trades; superb sailing winds blowing with remarkable steadiness in conditions that are neither too hot nor too cold. Coming generally from astern, and seldom blowing too strong in September, the north-east trades gave full freedom to each yacht to select where to aim for their passage through the doldrums ahead. They also gave full scope for hoisting all possible sail; this could be expected to benefit the eight ketches, which are all allowed to carry sails between their two masts without handicap penalty, they were specially eager to gain every mile they could in this way, as once into the south-east trades, the seven sloops and cutters, with their single masts, could be expected to better them when sailing close hauled into the wind.

The bulk of the fleet headed for much the same longitude of 21 degrees west to meet the doldrums in about 12 degrees north latitude. They were led by *Heath's Condor*, whose crew estimated that they were then 200 miles ahead; however the navigator of *Kings Legend* discovered as they reached the doldrums that his watch had been reading wrong, and actually he was only 18 miles north of *Heath's Condor* although some 50 miles further west, where she carried the trade winds further before meeting the doldrums.

Kings Legend had sailed fast through the north-east trades to keep on such good terms with the much bigger *Heath's Condor* and actually she was a few miles ahead of *G.B. II*, even bigger still. However, fast as she sailed she was overtaken one morning by four pilot whales while those on watch also sighted a 30 ft. shark basking in the sun. 'That shark was

immense' recorded the log which also mentioned 'we made off with haste'.

Close behind these three leaders came *Flyer*, then *ADC Accutrac* and *Disque D'Or* some 60 miles astern of her. Making to the westward, on the extreme right wing of the advancing front, having sailed through the Cape Verde Islands, was *Neptune*; she had much further to sail, but prayed that in the end she would prove to be in a strong windward position.

On the opposite wing of this 400 mile wide band and closest to the African coast as they reached the doldrums was *33 Export*, taking the shortest line for Cape Town and praying that the south-west monsoon from Africa would give a good lift, before the south-east trades headed her.

In spite of the Bay of Biscay calms, unexpected for late August, the whole fleet had made splendid time from Portsmouth to the doldrums. No rough weather or really strong winds had been experienced, and the wind direction had been generally favourable. However, it had been no easy time for crews as following and variable winds means frequent changes and continuous trimming of the sails.

Heath's Condor was first to the doldrums in 15 days, but by no means far enough ahead to save her time on handicap. The main trophies were to be awarded on handicap results so that the smallest, *Traite de Rome*, would beat *Heath's Condor* or *G.B. II*, even if several days behind her. The fleet had been kept bunched by the light conditions so that even *33 Export*, one of the smaller yachts which had also lost time by her call in Madeira, was less than three days behind.

It is only really possible to assess how one yacht stands relative to another when all have to round a particular point; but as they were free to spread out across the width of the Atlantic Ocean it could only be a matter of guesswork and ocean racing hunch during the race to place them in handicap order. Yet on reaching the doldrums *King's Legend* seemed very well placed, especially as she was a sloop

Repairing sails onboard *Adventure* was relatively pleasant work in the tropics.

which could expect to benefit from the stiff windward work of the south-east trades ahead.

However two big tactical puzzles, the doldrums and the South Atlantic High, were still ahead. Also there were over 3,000 miles of sailing to Cape Town, and much can happen to crews or yachts over that distance.

4 The Doldrums to South Africa

The doldrums, or to the meteorologists the inter-tropical front, form an uneasy belt between the North and South Atlantic Oceans. The weather becomes sultry and very hot, heavy rain is common, and the winds vary from practically nothing to heavy squalls, while their direction may be from all points of the compass. Thus *Flyer*'s log, recorded typically that it was like sailing in a hot house, and later referred to an unreal warm and humid world.

Sailing ships of old sometimes took two weeks or more to get through the doldrums, as they were slow to manoeuvre and often light handed, so at times a squall would be past before the ship had been turned and the sails trimmed to benefit from it. The muggy heat, combined with the conventionally dull diet at sea in those days added nothing to the alertness of the crews, and often the ship's bottom would be so foul with weed and barnacles that she would not move at all in the very light airs between the squalls.

A modern sailing yacht, with a full racing crew, is quite a different matter; so even if the conditions were depressing, the best of crews look upon the doldrums as a challenge through which they have to outdo their rivals.

Kings Legend first met the doldrums during the evening of 11 September, and spent a wet night with many wind shifts and sail changes, chasing squalls as much as her speed allowed,

so she managed to log ten miles in the four hours of the middle watch.

Flyer, not far behind, hit the doldrums an

Flyer nearly becalmed with her crew striving to gain every inch.

hour or two later in 11°10′ north latitude; she reported that she was just about becalmed for 13 hours but never lost steerage way nor logged less than nine miles in any 4-hour watch. Her navigator commented that the good food and time taken to enjoy it help in raising the spirits in otherwise demanding conditions; it is interesting that Cornelius van Rietschoten, her skipper, made no use of one of the old time methods of keeping up morale of a crew at sea—and perhaps a tot of rum would have slowed the quick reactions which he required for every minute of the night and day. Other skippers had different views, so some yachts ran a 'happy hour' in the dog watches, when the crew had a drink together; protagonists of

this feel that it helps to reduce the petty irritations that come from living in a cramped space. Whatever the technique all agree on the importance of crew compatibility, and also that this aspect needs special effort all round.

In her second night of the doldrums *Flyer* recorded exciting sailing in the squalls, with the boat at times over-pressed in their eagerness to get clear of the doldrums. This was effective as soon after midnight she recorded 'The fun of the line squalls is over and we are again sailing in light airs'. The rain had stopped after an eight hour downpour, and the dawn brought sunshine to dry out wet clothes, as the yacht sailed close hauled at seven knots.

Kings Legend worked her way quickly

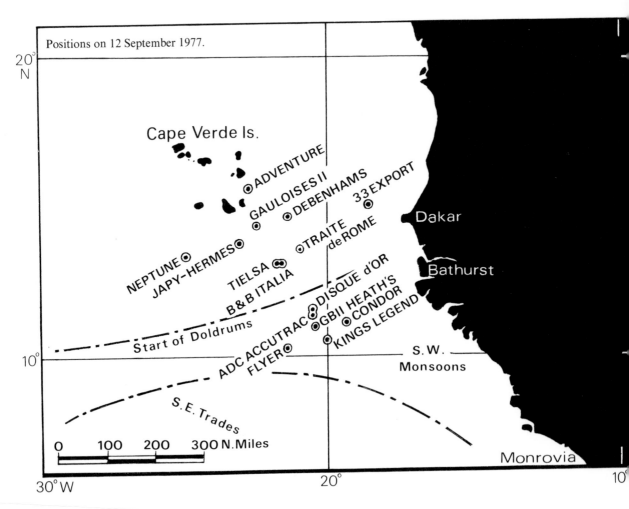

through the doldrums, only being badly delayed one day; however *Flyer* fared even better, and never dropped below 112 miles for noon to noon run. Once through that obstacle *Flyer* was actually ahead of *Kings Legend* and her log modestly suggests 'It might be possible that, for today, we are leading on handicap'. Actually, without even allowing for handicap, she was just about ahead of *Heath's Condor*, both being some three thousand miles away from Cape Town. Leslie Williams had taken *Heath's Condor* well east, towards the African coast; she had fared less well in the doldrums, meeting them sooner than the yachts further to the west, and enduring longer periods of frustrating conditions. Twice in succession one night she turned off her course and set a spinnaker trying without success to reach a squall with their promise of ample wind, but the third time she intercepted a fantastic rain squall with winds up to 30 knots, which gave her half a dozen miles of distance besides $8\frac{1}{2}$ gallons of fresh water.

G.B. II also had some bad doldrum days, besides some excitements in the squalls which must have seemed alarming enough to those with little experience of such conditions; two weeks at sea is enough to learn a great deal, but until then they had yet to contend with more than a fesh breeze. In five days she lost 100 miles and came out of the doldrums 85 miles astern of *Flyer*.

Perhaps the relatively smaller yachts might have some advantage in quick sail handling, but the luck of the squalls was uneven. Smallest of all, *Traite de Rome* came up to the doldrums in about the same longitude as *G.B. II* yet lost more than 100 miles on her in the process. *Adventure*, next smallest in size, kept to the westward, sighting the lighthouse on Sal Island in the Cape Verde group and then sailing almost due south to the doldrums. She caught up some 60 miles on *Traite de Rome*, but fared far less well than *Flyer*.

ADC Accutrac, following on a track some 50 miles nearer to Africa than *Flyer*, approached the doldrums about 60 miles behind her, but only got clear from the doldrums four days later, by which time she had lost 250 miles. Worst still for her was her special rival and sister ship *Disque D'Or*, as they reached the doldrums within 10 miles of each other, yet four days later they were 207 miles apart.

Was this all a matter of good luck for one and bad luck for another nearby? Certainly the doldrums play some devilish tricks, but maybe pure racing skill played a part in this too. *Disque D'Or* was skippered by a dinghy champion, with a couple more dinghy champions in his crew. They would be expert in gaining every possible foot out of capricious winds, and they would be accustomed, too, to strong gusts hurling down on the lakes from Swiss mountains. Cornelius van Rietschoten started his racing in dinghies and was thoroughly practiced in close racing techniques; *Flyer's* log in the doldrums, recorded that her crew were fighting for boat speed with the spinnaker sheets constantly in hand.

The log of *ADC Accutrac* gives a clue when it records 'Prepared to sit it out in the doldrums—hope it won't be too long'. No wonder that four swallows, probably migrating from West Africa to St. Helena or Ascension Island, preferred to adopt the more relaxed atmosphere of *ADC Accutrac*, which also had other visitors during the doldrums. She was buzzed by a French reconnaissance aircraft, so all hands came on deck to give a display of diving overboard; it turned out that the plane had been chartered by French news reporters, and their photos disclosed that the *à la mode* bathing wear for those waters was *au naturel*.

Meantime *Heath's Condor* was again well in the lead making reasonable speed with winds mostly south-westerly. At noon on 15 September she had less than a hundred miles to cross the equator and was expecting to pick up the steadier south-east trades at any time. The wind had freshened in the forenoon as a second reef had been taken in the mainsail, with a yankee and working staysail set forward; there was occasional drizzle.

Dr. David Dickson described what happened next from where he stood just behind Julian Gildersleeve at the wheel. Peter Blake had just appeared in the hatchway to ask about the state of weather and the sails set, when there was a grinding and crashing sound as the whole boat shook violently. Peter yelled 'The mast's gone' as he leapt on deck, then Dr. David Dickson looked up to see that the mast had broken between the masthead and the upper spreaders; the broken part was toppling down on the lee side, as it went causing another break just above the lower spreaders. The three sections were still held together by the halyards rove inside them.

All of a sudden it was raining shrouds and stays. The mast head fell over the lee side, making a hole through the hull a couple of feet above the waterline.

As the yacht was rolling heavily with no sail to steady her, it was fine seamanship indeed to have all cleared away and a jury rig set within

two hours. With no halyards left, Peter Blake was hoisted aloft on the spinnaker pole lift, and a halyard was rigged on a strap around the lower spreader; with this the genoa staysail was hoisted upside down, with its head as the tack. Then abaft the stump mast the reaching staysail was set with its foot as the luff. This made an effective down wind rig to give a speed of six knots, as Leslie Williams set a northeasterly course for Monrovia.

Two hours later *Heath's Condor* spoke on her radio to *Kings Legend*, asking that Robin Knox-Johnston be informed in England and stating that no assistance was needed. 'Poor old her', recorded the official log of *Kings Legend*. 'We know how she feels'.

With the nearest port 300 miles away, and some 3,000 miles from her base in England, anyone might assume that *Heath's Condor* was out of the race. That is if they did not know the powerful effect of Robin Knox-Johnston and Leslie Williams working together to overcome almost impossible obstacles. As the yachts sailed for harbour under jury rig

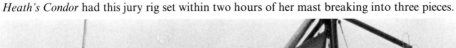

Heath's Condor had this jury rig set within two hours of her mast breaking into three pieces.

Leslie Williams and his crew were making hardwood plugs which could be screwed and glassed into the joins of the carbon fibre mast. With great ingenuity it was planned to build up in this way a temporary mast about the height of the original one up to the top spreaders. This could carry the storm mainsail and staysails, which would allow a reasonably efficient rig for the windward work to Cape Town, where the more permanent repairs could be made.

However, Robin Knox-Johnston back in England was working non-stop with fantastic energy and effectiveness. In almost no time at all he had a new aluminium mast ready and new rigging prepared. Then he arranged a charter flight to take the mast in three sections, together with all its equipment, out to Monrovia.

Nine days after the accident, well out in the Atlantic Ocean, Leslie Williams and his crew were assembling the new mast ashore and dressing it with the new rigging. Then the mast was moved to one of the ships in the port and

her derricks were borrowed to step it in *Heath's Condor*. That very evening she slipped, adjusting the rigging as she sailed back towards the position of the accident. Their seven days in harbour had been no rest cure, as it was the rainy season and work was intensive. Certainly they had a change in diet, but this was not all to the good as after sailing the doctor had half the crew as his patients with various degrees of food poisoning.

So *Heath's Condor* was back in the race.

The new mast, flown out to Monrovia in three sections, is stepped in *Heath's Condor* with the help of a ship's derricks. Movement of the ship and yacht in the swell made this a very tricky job.

Part of the broken glass fibre mast of *Heath's Condor*.

Yet on the day she left Monrovia, another competitor was putting back to sea from the other side of the Atlantic. This was the French *Japy-Hermes*, which Jimmy Viant had decided to turn from his course in mid-ocean and make for Recife in Brazil to land Patrick Therond after radio advice by a doctor member of the crew of *Gauloises II*. When sailing down wind the pain was tolerable, but when going to windward it again became so intense that there was no doubt about the wisdom of making for harbour. However once ashore, the treatment for his kidney stone was successful and Patrick Therond continued by plane to Cape Town, arriving thoroughly fit and able to continue onboard *Japy-Hermes* for the next leg.

The few hours spent in harbour allowed a slight relaxation for some of the crew while arrangements were being made for the patient. Yet it proved psychologically upsetting, and it took time to get back into the rhythm of hard racing. She was entitled by the race rules to take on provisions and equipment, but had no need for either. The actual diversion was not very great, as she planned a course well to the west, as indeed she had followed two years before in the Atlantic Triangle race to Cape Town. Yet even such a short delay put her into a different weather pattern from *Gauloises II*, which had previously been about level with her. Thus ten days after setting out from Recife she was flogging into a gale right on the nose, when *Gauloises II* was galloping along in excellent sailing conditions.

When *Heath's Condor* was dismasted in the lead we left *Kings Legend* and *Flyer* sailing with reefed mainsails hard on the wind, with *Kings Legend* steering south-east to a fresh southerly wind, planning to keep on the starboard tack until headed by the south-east trades.

Flyer, some 60 miles further west recorded at just the time of *Heath's Condor*'s accident, 'For the first time since the start the on watch is able to sit idle on deck'. No longer needing to keep spinnaker sheets in hand, besides frequent sail shifts, her organisation was modified so that in turn one man from each watch would have a day off. Next day the sky cleared and air dried, a swell came in from the south-east, and then fleecy trade wind clouds appeared again. She was in the south-east trades which were to be with her for 2½ weeks and nearly 3,000 miles of hard sailing.

She came close-hauled on the port tack, heading southwards, and aimed to skirt the South Atlantic High closely on its westward side, hoping that the wind would then free her for Cape Town. This was oilskin sailing, pounding into the seas, but the temperature was quite pleasant as they crossed the equator on the same tack a few hours later but on a track some 50 miles to windward. There was nothing between them, and both had identical handicaps. *Kings Legend*, as a sloop, might be considered to have a slight advantage for the tough windward work in the south-east trades, but so much would depend upon how their strategies worked out in circumventing the South Atlantic High.

G.B. II crossed the equator three hours after *Flyer*, but she was by then some 400 miles to the west, and therefore well to leeward.

The problem was to assess the High's position in two weeks time, and *Flyer* recorded as she crossed the equator that met. reports gave two different positions for it. Perhaps the truth was that in about 35°S there was a very large area of high pressure stretching over some 25 degrees of longitude. Within this plateau there may have been more than one area of very slightly higher pressure.

On 19 September *Flyer* sighted Ascension Island to port. Her crew were getting used to living at some 30° angle of heel, but at that time the trade winds were stable neither in strength or direction. There were fierce squalls, causing the main and mizzen to be reefed, and with the tough flog to windward they were finding it difficult to maintain racing concentration. *Kings Legend* also reported in this area that the wind varied in direction by 40° and in strength from 15 to 28 knots. She had a substantial leak

Japy-Hermes turned for Brazil to land an ill member of the crew; then sailed again into a different weather pattern from the rest of the fleet.

somewhere forward in the boat so had to spend effort in tracing it, but on 20 September assessed that she was lying equal first with *Flyer*. That day her run was 207 miles, while *Flyer* logged 214 miles and felt she was just pulling ahead.

ADC Accutrac crossed the equator three days after the three leaders, but her handicap put her ahead of *G.B. II*. She records at that time that sails had to be lowered to tension the backstay bottle screws as the hydraulic system had failed. This gave an opportunity to pay respects to King Neptune but it knocked several miles off her run for that watch. Her main engine failed due to a fuel injection pump fault, and the auxiliary generator was running short of fuel needed for battery charging; torches had to be used instead of the yacht's lighting system, so that enough power was available for the daily messages from Clare Francis for broadcasting on London's radio.

Adventure crossed the equator on 21 September, the day after *ADC Accutrac, Traite de Rome* and *Japy-Hermes*; King Neptune boarded *Adventure* at the precise moment of the 'equatorial transit' and in sparkling conditions had the skipper and four others introduced to him in the traditional method.

Flyer showed quite remarkable ability to windward for a ketch when beating against the south-east trades, her run on four successive days exceeded 200 miles. totalling 840 miles. She was using a reefed mainsail and a mizzen throughout, normally with one headsail; this was mainly No. 1 heavy genoa, which was under severe strain in the squalls but was excellent in between. It was wet work on deck, but down below the good food and comfortable living kept the crew going well.

In those four days the sloop *Kings Legend* covered 800 miles, while she had also edged up to windward on her special rival; through most of this she had two reefs in her mainsail, with No. 2 jib and forestaysail.

G.B. II, the biggest yacht in the race, made a splendid distance of 916 miles in those four days to 21 September. She made more sail shifts with her crew of 17, reefing and unreefing the main, hoisting and lowering the mizzen, and ringing the changes between No. 3 and 4 genoas. Her strategy was to sail with the apparent wind about 45° on the bow, and this brought her over 500 miles to leeward of *Kings Legend*, although which track would benefit depended upon the position of the high pressure area ahead.

This was becoming a critical matter for the three leaders, and of growing importance for all; *Neptune* and *Gauloises II* were to the west, with the rest of the fleet taking course between them and *Adventure*, which was edging over to the east.

On 22 September *Flyer* recorded that the race between her and *Kings Legend* was really on. The wind was definitely lighter and the squalls less severe. 'We assume we are the same distance to Cape Town. All systems go and an excellent steak for dinner'.

Still the barometer rose and still no signs of the wind freeing. Estimates for the position of the South Atlantic High seemed to show that it was moving rapidly and as atmospheric conditions interfered with the radio met. reports, each yacht feared that it was determined to block them. However one thing seemed just about as good a bet as any, and this was the team competition for the Long John prize. The three leading yachts had all been drawn in the team of *Kings Legend, Flyer* and *Disque D'Or*.

By 26 November, still with no change of wind direction in 31° south, and the High apparently south of its expected position, the crew of *Flyer* was getting anxious that *Kings Legend*'s more easterly position would put her right in the lead if the wind failed to change as forecast. By that time she was frequently reefing and unreefing the mainsail to adjust the angle of heel, to which *Flyer* is very sensitive.

On board *Kings Legend* the view was obviously different. 'This should hurt *Flyer*, according to plan', and by noon on 26 September she recorded 'We are well ahead now if

Flyer should tack. She must pray for a header'.

Yet slowly there were signs of wind freeing, and next morning *Flyer* tacked. Then it moved back the other way and *Kings Legend* recorded 'Headed. If *Flyer* has this wind and tacks she will pass very close. Damn'.

That is just what happened.

Six hours later, it was 20.30 on 27 September, *Flyer* passed under the stern of *Kings Legend*, which tacked on her weather quarter.

Five thousand miles and 31 days of hard racing. Two yachts with different rigs, yet identical handicaps. Yet they were almost close enough to shout. There was still another thousand miles to Cape Town, and it was clearly to be a race right to the finish.

At this time *G.B. II* was still sailing southwards, hoping for the westerly winds around the bottom of the high pressure. But she was right out of luck. On 28 September her log records dolefully 'And so we sailed into the South Atlantic High!' Wind force 1, variable, was the best that came to her for two days, and in one day she dropped to a mere 71 mile run, less than her worst day in the doldrums, and only one mile more than her worst in the Bay of Biscay calms. After four days of this, it was then 1 October, came the plea 'Oh Westerlies, where is your strength?' but at last this was answered with a brisk north-westerly wind which sent her tramping.

Perhaps her prayer had been too intense.

On the second night of fresh north-westerly winds, *G.B. II* was running at a good nine knots a compass course with spinnaker and mizzen staysail set. Around 3 a.m. the wind headed so the helmsman called the skipper. Robert James came on deck and took the wheel saying 'I think you can hold it', referring to the shy spinnaker. He was concentrating on the spinnaker trim, so just for a few moments was distracted from the wheel.

That was enough for the westerlies to show their strength, as a large wave caught her and the 77 ft. of yacht slewed round in a broach. She was pressed over until the lee deck was awash

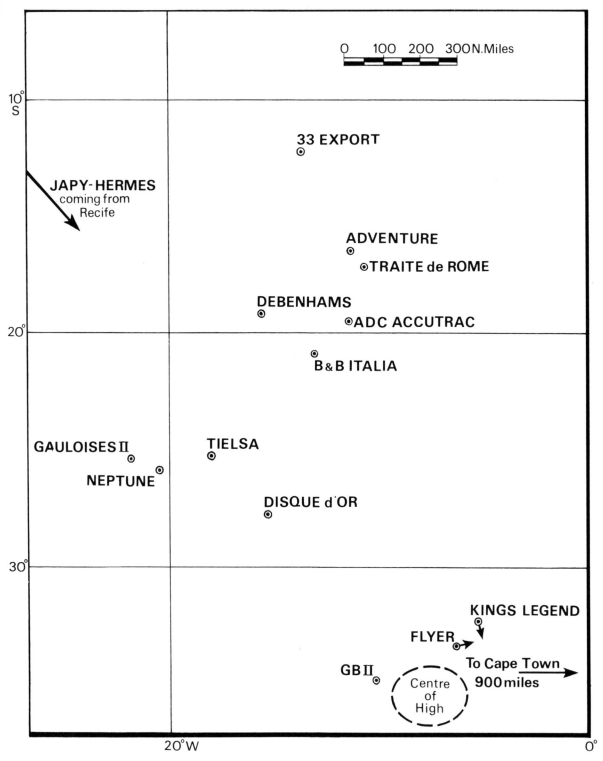

On 27 September the fleet was in the south-east trades, with the leaders beginning to feel the influence of the South Atlantic High.

57

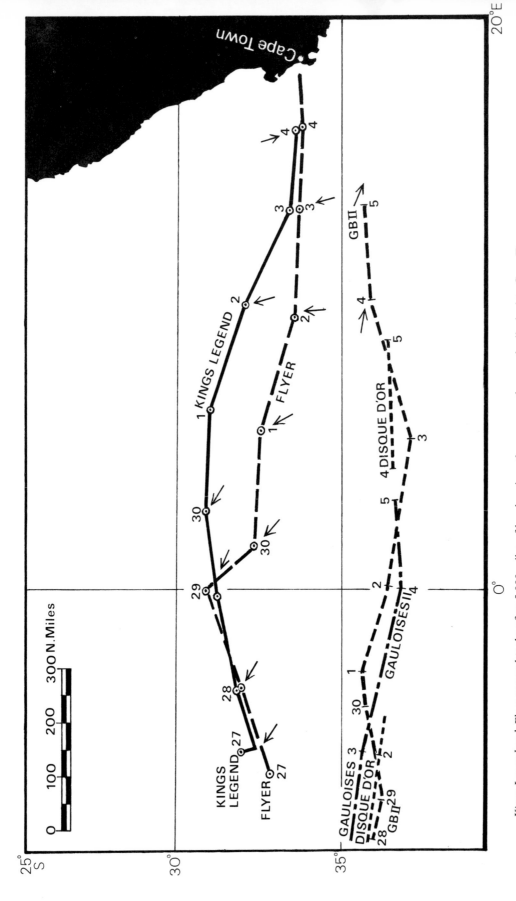

Kings Legend and *Flyer* crossed tacks after 5,000 miles of hard racing; then came a thousand mile duel to Cape Town, with *Great Britain II*, *Disque D'Or* and *Gauloises* challenging from the south.

with the spinnaker out of control in the water. For some 30 seconds she lay over, as unwelcome an experience to those down below as the watch on deck.

Then she righted herself, and it was an hour in the dark before the spinnaker was recovered, the crew could confirm that there was no damage and the problems were sorted out. In Cape Town after the finish Robert James commented wryly to race chairman, Admiral Steiner, 'A salutary lesson on steering down wind before we try the Southern Ocean'.

Both *Neptune* and *Gauloises II* took a westerly route, adding a good many miles to the distance sailed, but successfully sailing round the high pressure area to find the westerlies. *Neptune* actually went as far south as the island of Tristan da Cunha, but *Gauloises II* cut the corner just inside her to get just ahead on 3 October. Yet this wide detour, normally recommended as the best route, did not pay off as they were then the same distance from Cape Town as *Kings Legend* had been when she met *Flyer*. That was six days earlier, making a bigger margin than the 10 foot difference in rating between *Gauloises II* and the leading pair. Surely the amazing ability to windward of these superb big yachts allows new conceptions of ocean strategy.

Back then to the leading pair as they raced boat against boat from the evening of 27 September. They were still close hauled in the south-easterlies, with *Kings Legend* just ahead and planning to keep *Flyer* in sight.

Next day *Kings Legend* recorded that surprisingly the ketch was sailing higher than her at the same speed. The wind had increased to force 6, gusting to strong in prolonged squalls with rain, while the heavy swell seemed to be stopping *Kings Legend* more than *Flyer*, which by evening was 4 miles ahead. However it was consolation to know from the inter-yacht radio that *G.B. II* was 'parked' in the High.

Next morning, 29 September, the yachts were out of sight as each tacked with the heading windshifts. It was still blowing hard from the direction of Cape Town. 'Most uncomfortable' wrote *Kings Legend.*

That evening *Flyer* sighted a masthead light. It was ahead, and once more the pair crossed tacks, but this time *Kings Legend* held her starboard tack, which took her nearest to the course for Cape Town, while *Flyer* gambled on taking the port tack in her search for those westerlies.

30 September brought little change in conditions for either of the leaders. At 5 a.m. *Flyer* came round to the same tack as *Kings Legend*, but 90 miles south of her and 45 miles further away from Cape Town.

That night *Flyer* experienced a slight freeing of the wind, her crew enjoyed an easing of the motion after all the crashing and banging of the previous days. At 5 a.m. on 1 October, an excited note in the log 'On course for Cape Town'; yet at just the same time *Kings Legend* logged 'Prayers answered. Now on course for Cape Town'. There were still 600 miles to go.

Still no westerlies for either, but a moderate south-south-east wind allowed the sheets to be eased. The sky cleared, allowing accurate positions to be calculated, and the sun helped to dry the yachts.

'*Flyer* should not catch us now if the wind holds' recorded *Kings Legend*, while *Flyer*'s crew wondered whether they would still have a chance to cash in on their southerly position, but were not quite certain of their rival's position.

At last *Flyer* began to earn some benefit from her southing, when on the morning of 2 October her wind veered to south, while *Kings Legend* was to get another 20 hours of south-south-east, blowing as much as force 6. By noon, still some 90 miles to the south, *Flyer* was again in the lead—just five miles closer to the finish. Her log mentioned the difficulty of concentrating on sail trim and boat speed after such a long time at sea.

The crew of *Kings Legend* were in much the same situation. Afterwards some mentioned constipation, which they connected with running out of beer; and feelings sometimes became raw in those last intensive days. There was no shortage of food, but perhaps more roughage and green vegetables would have helped.

Next day, 3 October, the wind fell light for both as their course converged so that at noon they were some 10 miles apart, with *Flyer* just three miles in the lead, yet in the next four hours she logged only six miles, while *Kings Legend* logged one mile less. 220 miles to go and it did not help to hear that *Gauloises II* was running before the westerlies at 10 knots, even if she was over 800 miles astern.

'Agony' recorded *Kings Legend* next morning as *Flyer* was spotted from the masthead eight miles on her starboard bow. The sighting was reciprocated, so feelings were good onboard *Flyer*; 'ketch weather', she recorded, 'and we make good use of our staysails which *K.L.* does not carry'.

Their wind, still light, had come in from the north, and *Flyer* gybed several times to keep her position between Cape Town and their rival on which they kept a careful eye from the masthead; a hole in the wind and she could get by.

Before midnight the blink of Green Point lighthouse was sighted. 30 miles to go; *Flyer* recorded 'Wind is leaving us and conditions are very tricky', while at the same time *Kings Legend* wrote 'Our only hope is light wind'. *Gauloises II*, with her big handicap allowance, was a worry as well when the minutes dragged by with Cape Town clearly visible quite a distance away.

At last came the finish, with jubilation for the crew of *Flyer*, and great disappointment onboard *Kings Legend* 12 miles astern; yet it was she that sent the first congratulations, by radio; 'very much appreciated' recorded *Flyer*.

Just two hours between them after 38 days. This was real ocean racing.

Kings Legend crosses the line off Cape Town.

5 Pause in Cape Town

Cape Town is rightly proud of the welcome and hospitality it affords to seafarers of all nations, and with good reason calls itself the 'Tavern of the Seas'; sailors, provided they are 'seaman in transit', are allowed ashore at will, regardless of creed, colour, nationality or politics; and providing that they leave with their ships.

Flyer, quickly followed by *Kings Legend*, was timed across the finish line by the Cruising Association of South Africa, which undertook all matters connected with the finish and re-start at Cape Town, besides the slipping and repair of yachts and gear, the refreshment of crews and assistance in dealing with local authorities such as Customs, Immigration and Health in conjunction with the Royal Cape Yacht Club.

Once finished, they were each in turn guided to berths by Peter Niehams, outside manager of the Royal Cape Yacht Club, which was the host club and social centre from the stop-over. These two clubs were well geared to the needs of major international yachting, having previously handled such events as the Cape to Rio race, the Atlantic Triangle and the first *Whitbread* race.

Adjoining the R.C.Y.C. is S.A.S. *Unitie*, Headquarters of the South African Naval

Letters from home as soon as *Flyer* berths off the Royal Cape Yacht Club.

Reserve, where a wide range of services to yachts were available, including extra mooring, medical attention, besides additional washing facilities for their crews. Another valuable asset was the spotless floor for spreading out sails to be repaired, while the parade ground had sprouted an assembly of huts for temporary stowage of yacht gear, laundry, reception and race offices and so forth.

The whole Cape Town organisation for the race was co-ordinated by a special committee, presided over by Basil Linhorst, the R.N.S.A.'s Honorary Local Officer and a past Commodore of the R.C.Y.C., while also present at Cape Town was a section of the central R.N.S.A. Race Committee, under its chairman Admiral Steiner, who personally boarded each yacht on arrival to advise crews in clearing Customs, Health and Immigration authorities. Those who arrived and were to leave in the racing yachts were treated as 'Seamen in transit', for whom the formalities were minimal; but where crew changes were involved a more elaborate procedure was obviously needed.

On arrival at her berth alongside a pontoon off the R.C.Y.C. *Flyer* was contacted by the Rondebosch Rotary Club which had adopted her for recreational and other hospitality. In the same way *Kings Legend*'s host was the Parow Rotary Club, and each yacht on arrival had a Rotary Club as host, with a named contact available in his office or at home.

The overall impression was of a red-hot welcome, with the offer of so much hospitality that problems earmarked for immediate attention while at sea might well be forgotten for a day or so. Indeed the crews of the first two finishers had hardly adjusted to a life without night watches when *G.B. II* sailed in to cross the line just over 32 hours after *Flyer*; that was about the time which *G.B. II* had spent parked in the South Atlantic High. She had made a fine passage from Portsmouth, actually three days faster than her first *Whitbread* race four years before with a crew of picked paratroopers, although this time some of her crew had never sailed before. To some of these her middle watch broach, when the wind returned after she escaped from the High, had left a strong impression, and the story gleaned from them by newsmen ashore was a good deal more lurid than the factual account of such a thoroughly experienced seaman as Robert James, for

In Cape Town harbour, with the table mountain behind.

whom the broach was a waste of valuable minutes with no damage done.

A day later came *Disque D'Or* which had taken a course almost precisely through the spot where *G.B. II* had been becalmed in the High, yet was carried through it speedily by the westerlies which had by then taken over.

Two days later again, it was 9 October, three yachts made the finish. First came *Tielsa*, which had taken a course furthest south of all to ensure she avoided the High, and she seemed to be seeking a pre-view of the Roaring Forties. Then came *Gauloises II* whose wide detour to the west, following the traditional clipper route, gave a slow passage across the equator, although in the last two thousand miles she made such speed that her finish time gave her third place on corrected time, less than 30 hours behind the winner.

Meantime there had been another neck and neck duel for the finish, as on 7 October *ADC Accutrac* sighted *Neptune* to the south with Cape Town some 350 miles away. All day they had struggled against each other, and all through the night as well; yet when dawn came next day they were out of sight of each other as *Neptune* had edged southwards. This did not serve her so well and *ADC* got well ahead to cross the line less than an hour and a half after *Gauloises II*, while *Neptune* arrived next morning some 15 hours later.

That day and the next *B & B Italia*, *Adventure*, *Debenhams* and *Traite de Rome* all finished. There had been yet another duel for the line for the last few hundred miles between *Traite de Rome* and *Adventure*, and although the E.E.C. multi-lingual crew was to get the best of it on handicap, *Adventure*'s crew had the satisfaction of finishing a few hours ahead. Both crews perhaps had the added incentive of getting thirsty; *Adventure*'s fresh water tanks had run dry three days before, following a leak, and since then she had depended only on a few gallons of emergency water, plus a small quantity of rain water collected weeks before in the doldrums. It was when each man and

woman was down to half rations of water that *Adventure* recorded her best day's run since leaving Portsmouth; however it was at the expense of a spinnaker blown out. *Traite de Rome* had a similar problem of water shortage, and was completely out of beer or wine; she had three spinnakers blown out in the leg from Portsmouth.

Thus six days after the first yacht crossed the line 12 had finished, leaving only the three which had been forced to interrupt their voyages with harbour calls. This influx of large yachts so close together meant that a highly concentrated effort was needed by the reception organisation, with Tom Unite, secretary of the Capetown Committee besides his normal task as secretary of the C.A.S.A., working day and night.

It also meant that Admiral Steiner's race committee had to decide upon the start date for the next leg, as the rules required that when 70% of those entered for the next leg had arrived the decision should be made for a date between five and 14 days later. It was a decision that needed careful thought, weighing of all the factors affecting each competitor. *Heath's Condor*, *Japy-Hermes* and *33 Export* had still to arrive, so the time they would need to prepare for the tough Southern Ocean leg ahead was still partly conjecture; there was also consideration of the probable load on the shipping and yacht servicing facilities ashore. Then a third consideration was that the first leg had been sailed very fast, so it was still only spring in the Southern Ocean, with darkness lasting for several hours in the area where yachts might encounter icebergs.

The state of the crews, as well as the yachts, had to be taken into account, but here there was no problem. Dr. Baigrie, Principal Surgeon of the Groote Schuur Hospital and honorary medical officer on the Cape Town committee, reported that the race crews were exceptionally fit in mind and body, with no incidence of serious injury in the whole fleet. He noted that someone about whose fitness to sail at all there had been reasonable doubt before leaving Portsmouth, obliged him by climbing to the cross trees, hand over hand, after arrival at Cape Town. Patients who had psychological and related problems prior to sailing were free of them after arrival.

After assessing all these factors the decision was made to re-start the race on 25 October, so Angela Peacop and Yvonne Peiser, who in Cape Town both did valuable voluntary work helping the main race committee from Britain, typed out this information and distributed it to the yachts and everyone else concerned.

This was the signal for Eric Fry and his team of scrutineers to get to work, carefully checking that each yacht still complied with the needs of the compulsory equipment besides the special regulations imposed for the race; thus life raft certificates had to be checked as still valid, fire extinguishers noted and personal safety harness examined for each member of the crew. There were numerous other items to be ticked off on the list prepared for each yacht, and overall came the technical decision that each hull was still capable of withstanding solid water and knock-down.

Five days went by before the next two yachts arrived. *Heath's Condor* had made fine speed after setting out from Monrovia with her new mast, in spite of the problems of adjusting the rigging and also meeting right on the nose a gale which surprisingly blew up with a high barometer steadily rising. However, her position was fully reported, so her arrival could be foretold correctly, and in Cape Town she did not need to slip; indeed Leslie Williams and his crew had her almost ready to start the next leg straight away.

About an hour ahead of her came *33 Export*, which was something of a relief as radio failure meant that there had been no contact with her for some three weeks. Indeed this lack of knowledge about her whereabouts was diversified by some to the expression 'missing', which to seamen, and most interested laymen too, can have quite a different meaning. Thus

air exercises were conducted, but the South Atlantic Ocean is a vast area in which to find a yacht whose last reported position was in the tropics, and it is not a bit surprising that she was not seen.

The failure of her radio reporting was a matter of inability to generate electric power. This was due to the loosening of the nuts holding a pump which fell into the sump, while the engine oil drained into the gear-box. The power failure also meant no electric instruments and candle light down below.

Disque D'Or had also been out of radio touch when she arrived nine days earlier, but in her case flooding back through the exhaust system had disabled the engine. With no means of generating electricity she also had other problems and she arrived using oil navigation and cabin lights. *ADC Accutrac* had been another yacht to suffer engine trouble which hindered radio communications. However a small charging engine could produce enough power for Clare Francis' calls to get through to Capital Radio in London, where they could be passed on to Race Control Headquarters; but these meant that Bumble had to cook by torchlight or candles.

Apart from the engine and radio repair necessary in *33 Export*, she required more attention on arrival than any other yacht, with the need to unstep the mast, beef up the rigging, fit a bigger wheel and also carry out some welding to replace a temporary shroud plate bolted to the hull during a gale of 45 knots.

It was made clear to *33 Export* that she could not be allowed to start the next leg until she was completely fit for the weather that might be expected in the Southern Ocean. Alain Gabbay fully appreciated this and made it a challenge to work flat out until all was completed. It is to the great credit of he and his crew, especially considering the difficult conditions under which they had been sailing for three weeks, that everything was done and they were able to start with the fleet only nine days after arrival. They were greatly helped by Martin

Francis who had flown from Paris to assist.

Several yachts had difficulty in contacting shore radio stations while enjoying excellent radio communications on the inter-yacht frequency. Thus it sometimes happened that the best information about yachts still at sea came from yachts in harbour which continued to keep watch on the 'children's hour'.

Two days after *Heath's Condor* came *Japy-Hermes*, and the fleet was complete at Cape Town. We have already told how Jimmy Viant decided to make for Recife in Brazil to land a crew man after medical diagnosis from a doctor in *Gauloises II*; also how this diversion put her into a different weather pattern giving her a gale on the nose and much hard sailing. Inevitably this put her back many days, but it was excellent seamanship all round that she arrived in fine shape with only the need to slip for a bottom clean before being ready to re-start.

The Yacht Services office, under Werner Weinlig, strategically placed at the foot of the pontoons, was kept particularly busy. Slipping of the yachts for underwater repairs and bottom cleaning was quite a problem for George Meek with time so limited when some needed fairly extensive work. The R.C.Y.C. cradle could be used for the smaller yachts, but those with larger beams had to be lifted out, and the lift could only handle one at a time. Almost inevitably some crews found on examination out of the water that more work was needed than had been expected, especially due to rudder troubles: for instance *Gauloises II* fitted a new rudder. Some of those whose only need was to scrub their bottoms clean had to be hurried back into the water although keen crews would have liked a little longer to burnish the hull for that fractional extra speed. A point noticed was that scarcely any goose barnacles had grown on white anti-fouling, many were on red and a profusion on blue; was this colour preference by these cirripeds, or was it a matter of the chemical composition in which the colour was incidental?

Probably the problem of victualling for the cold, rough leg to follow was as important as anything, and at times as complicated too. Some yachts had arranged for nearly all their food to be shipped out from their home countries, and their anxiety grew when the shipments had not arrived a few days before the start. Hamish Weares spent hours in one of the race offices in S.A.S. Unitie trying to trace shipments, and also assisting the formalities of any of the crews who were leaving the yachts in Cape Town, besides the new ones who were joining. He also dragged out of skippers, usually too involved with other matters to have much time for paper work, complete new crew lists with photographs of any newcomer.

Prizegiving for the first leg was held in S.A.S. Unitie soon after all the yachts had arrived. A distinguished gathering of 600 people was present when trophies for each yacht were handed out by Mrs Dickie Lindhorst, wife of

The need to slip for underwater repairs was a major factor in assessing the time at stopovers.

The skippers attend a briefing for the leg to Auckland. From left to right—standing—Jimmy Viant (*Japy-Hermes*), Robin Knox-Johnston (*Heath's Condor*), Philippe Hanin (*Traite de Rome*), Clare Francis (*ADC Accutrac*), Eric Loizeau (*Gauloises II*), John Ridgway (*Debenhams*), Dirk Nauta (*Tielsa*), Cornelius van Riets-choten (*Flyer*), David Leslie (*Adventure*), Pierre Fehlmann (*Disque D'Or*), Corrado di Majo (*B & B Italia*); crouching—Robert James (*Great Britain II*), Bernard Deguy (*Neptune*), Mike Clancy (*Kings Legend*), Alain Gabbay (*33 Export*).

the Cape Town Committee's chairman. Six hundred voices made abundantly clear their popular approval when Cornelius van Rietschoten was awarded the prize for *Flyer*'s win on corrected time.

This trophy had been presented by the City Council of Cape Town, and on behalf of the Mayor, who had collapsed from overwork soon after the first yachts came in, the Deputy Mayor spoke of the courage and sense of adventure shown by the crews.

On the eve of the start came the briefing of all skippers and navigators. The sailing instructions for the next leg were presented—the course was simply from Cape Town by any route seaward to Auckland—and the opportunity given for any questions of the Race Committee. The hazards of the Agulhas Cur-

rent were stressed, with the advice to get south as quickly as possible; indeed when gales storm over this fast running current which runs all along the southern coast of South Africa, seas can be so exceptionally dangerous that this area has been the graveyard of many large ships.

Fortunately the weather forecast at the briefing was entirely favourable, giving every chance for the yachts to get south of the Agulhas current before any gale struck them. The best of crews is likely to be rather vulnerable to seasickness during the first day or so at sea after the hospitality of Cape Town.

Thus by the morning of 25 October all yachts were ready, and every crew member had a very good idea of the tough conditions they could expect during the next leg of 7,400 miles.

6 Southern Ocean to New Zealand

All 15 yachts cast off their lines from Cape Town and steered out into Table Bay on the morning of 25 October 1977. The warm sunshine helped to keep the thoughts of those onboard tied to friendly faces long after they had faded into the distant background; 'the atmosphere was unusually quiet onboard', logged *Flyer*.

The yachts gathered around No 1 Fairway buoy as a warning gun was fired from a committee boat at 1.15 p.m. Fifteen minutes later all flags were hauled down with the final gun, and they were off, beating into a light wind from the southwards. 'From Cape Town by any sea route to Auckland. Handicap distance 7,400', read the race instructions, and as the crew came to life with the need to shift sails and trim the sheets, thoughts wandered momentarily to the gales, snow and ice that lay ahead.

Very few of those onboard had previously ventured under sail into the Roaring Forties, but they had all read fearsome accounts of these from the clipper age. Fewer still had been down to the Fifties, which has traditionally been considered so storm ridden as to be hazardous for navigation under sail, and only to be entered when forced southwards round Cape Horn.

However, one man in the racing fleet knew the Southern Ocean perhaps as well as any one alive. He was Captain Tom Woodfield, formerly Master of the Antarctic Research Ships *Shackleton, John Biscoe* and *Bransfield*; but on leaving Cape Town that day, he was navigator of the yacht *Debenhams*.

He was a professional seaman who had spent most of his working life in the south and was also an adviser to the race committee; so he felt it only right to offer some notes on his experience for the use of his competitors in the

The race re-starts off Cape Town—next stop New Zealand.

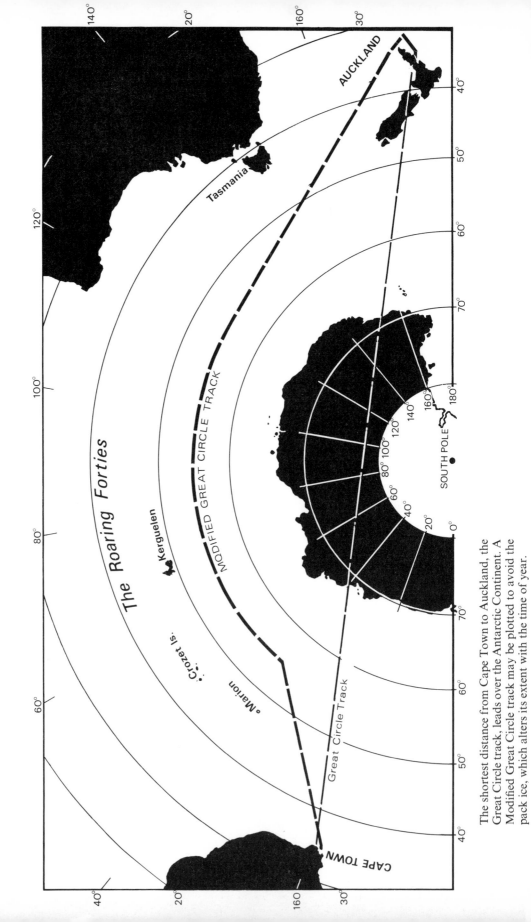

The shortest distance from Cape Town to Auckland, the Great Circle track, leads over the Antarctic Continent. A Modified Great Circle track may be plotted to avoid the pack ice, which alters its extent with the time of year.

other yachts. The usual advice, such as given in the *Ocean Passage of the World*, is to keep scarcely southwards of 40° latitude; yet Tom Woodfield recommended a far more southerly course, perhaps going down to 55° south. He suggested that it would not be very much colder, and the weather would normally be no worse; indeed he reported that the fiercest seas were less dependent upon the latitude than upon shallow water, such as the notorious Agulhas Bank, and waters around the islands of Marion, Crozet, Kerguelen and Heard.

He warned that ice would more frequently be met on a southerly track, but suggested that there should be no difficulty in avoiding icebergs so long as they were visible. At the time they were sailing that leg of the course, he pointed out, the twilight lasted much longer in 55° than in 40° south latitude, and nights were far shorter.

The southerly course is also shorter as, due to the earth's curvature, the shortest line from the Cape of Good Hope to the northern tip of New Zealand crosses the land of the Antarctic continent in about 70° south. This shortest line

between two points is known to seamen as the Great Circle, and the closer a vessel keeps to it, the shorter is the distance.

Tom Woodfield advised that an early aim should be to get south clear of the Agulhas Bank, over which a gale blowing against the fast current may cause particularly dangerous seas; even vast tankers two thousand times bigger than the racing yachts have been seriously damaged in this area. Apart from this hazard, should a gale blow up, there was every advantage in getting across this contrary current as soon as possible, even if initially the course was more to the east than to the west.

The yachts spent that first day beating slowly out of Table Bay towards the Cape of Good Hope. *Kings Legend* nosed out a counter current close inshore and made the most of it, but for all progress was slow and Robert James could well record in the log of *G.B.II* 'So much for the Cape of Storms'; yet he well knew how the Cape of Good Hope could earn this evil reputation at times.

'Nothing too strong to upset the stomach' recorded the log of *ADC Accutrac*, and crews in

Cape of Good Hope—famous as the Cape of Storms, with False Bay beyond.

several yachts found that the quiet weather gave them a chance to catch up on sleep after the whirl of Cape Town. For many, another day passed before the crews had fully gathered their wits together. By that time *Kings Legend* was well in the lead, sailing to a moderate breeze from the south-east. Her special rival, Dutch *Flyer*, was at noon some 40 miles to the west of her and pretty much becalmed as yachts came up over the horizon all day. 'We appear to have a private patch of calm', she recorded next day, 27 October, having covered only 70 miles compared with 156 miles by *Kings Legend*. Yet it was not really a private calm as her fellow Dutch yacht *Tielsa* covered only 67 miles in the same time; *Traite de Rome* and Swiss *Disque D'Or* did little better, while both the maxi-yachts *G.B.II* and *Heath's Condor* made good only 100 miles.

Thus when the wind shifted westerly with the first of the passing fronts *Kings Legend* had a lead of nearly 50 miles, and the rest of the fleet was spread out astern of her.

Then came the first gale to blow away the very last of the cobwebs before the fleet got south to the Roaring Forties. It was a short one, but on the night of 28 October *G.B.II* reported 'Big squall' and as the wind blew for an hour at force 8 she shortened sail to a single reef in the mainsail and No 3 genoa. The wind reached *ADC Accutrac* earlier and she was caught out by a frontal squall with her working spinnaker set; the strain pulled out a deck fitting, her spinnaker pole skied and this led to 'an interesting broach, first to windward, then to leeward'. The spinnaker was recovered undamaged but, unfortunately, her best genoa in its bag was washed overboard and lost. Later that day, when the wind temporarily eased, she set her starcut spinnaker; as the wind freshened again this spinnaker blew out, leaving just a small sector at the masthead to be recovered later by a climb aloft.

Japy-Hermes also blew out a spinnaker, besides her big boy, while *Neptune* broke two spinnaker poles. *Adventure* ripped her big boy,

and while recovering it passed *Gauloises II*, which had previously been sailing neck and neck with her but was then stopped and lying a-hull, with the wind blowing 40–45 knots. It was many hours later before the crew of *Adventure* knew the reason why.

Gauloises II had been worst hit of any, and the reason that she lay stopped was that she was rudderless. After Eric Loizeau had skippered her into third place in the leg to Cape Town, he decided to replace her rudder with a stronger one before the Southern Ocean legs began; it was this rudder which had been broken off by the seas. Well might she log the sea as 'forte', as she set sail again, using her emergency rudder hung from the transom, to make back to South Africa; she reached Port Elizabeth two days later. Meantime, so it was reported, the skipper's fiancée jumped into an aeroplane with the replacement rudder 'under her arm' and arrived in Port Elizabeth a few hours before the yacht. A very quick change was made, and that same day *Gauloises II* was back in the race; yet the days lost since her accident and the need to regain distance to the south, put her into a different weather pattern from the rest of the fleet, and she was to encounter far more severe conditions.

On 29 October, the day following the loss of *Gauloises II*'s rudder, *Kings Legend* was hit by a heavy squall when a cold front passed. Billy Porter was washed aft into the shrouds and injured his right hip bone enough to incapacitate him for a time; also during a further broach some item of gear flying across the cabin gashed the forehead of another of the crew. Then soon after that Mike Clancy, the skipper, suffered a severe back injury on a spinnaker sheet; this was to keep him below for several days.

These blows were a prelude to the Roaring Forties and further south; perhaps they were a valuable warning of the power of the wind and

Skip Novak, navigator of *Kings Legend*, takes the wheel on a drying out day after the blow.

sea, as more damage was suffered then than in the more protracted blows that were to come further south. Certainly they must lend weight to the advice of Tom Woodfield that there is little benefit in trying to keep to a track of around 40° south latitude.

The strong winds brought *Heath's Condor* into her own. She was sailing more than 250 miles a day 'Going like the clappers' she logged, with her sights set on *Kings Legend* still ahead. Two spinnakers damaged kept Paul Newell hard at it sewing, and spinnaker guys were being repaired by splicing, while David Alan-Williams went aloft to retrieve a parted halyard. Next day all was in order for any further gale.

Reward for this pressure of work came to *Heath's Condor* that evening—30 October—with the sighting of a light on the beam. This was confirmed as *Kings Legend* before it dropped astern, with her crew partly handicapped by injuries.

Once *Heath's Condor* had gained the lead she was to hold it all the way to Auckland. Her strategy was to take the Great Circle down to latitude 55° south, then sail along that latitude to 120° east; from there to take the Great Circle for Cape Ringa, New Zealand. However, as *Heath's Condor* took the lead in actual position, *Adventure* gained the best place on handicap; she had kept up top speed as sail was reduced in the gale to two reefs in the mainsail, with a jib poled out on the other side and she reported surfing at up to 20 knots, to give a day's run on 30 October which easily beat her previous best.

By that same day *Debenhams* was already down to 44°S; she placed ice lookouts on the advice of Tom Woodfield, who himself spent many cold hours clinging to the weather shrouds as the best lookout position. *Debenhams* was the only yacht to pass south of Marion Island, from which excellent weather forecasts were broadcast in plain language to the fleet until all the yachts were many hundred miles past it. The yachtsmen developed a warm

feeling for the small party of scientists on this isolated island, who took such active interest in their progress. 'Very kind of their operators' logged *Flyer*.

Some 650 miles east of Marion Island lie the uninhabited Crozet Islands, and passing it the fleet had divided into two, the Dutch pair *Flyer* and *Tielsa*, the French trio *Neptune, Japy-Hermes* and *33 Export*, besides British *ADC Accutrac*, all kept north of these islands, which were sighted by all of them except *Flyer*, which passed well to the north. *ADC Accutrac* also gave the islands a wide berth, due to thick fog with visibility down to 100 yards; however, in a gap between the fog banks she caught a glimpse of the land 20 miles off.

This northerly group was not faring too well with the wind, as a high pressure area held them. 'More wind please' logged *Flyer*, and mentioned a remarkable sunrise with an absolutely clear sky; her log also told about plenty of birds, some kelp and porpoises. 'All sails have been repaired. We are so used to the high galley standards that it is hardly mentioned in the log any more'. Both *Neptune* and *Tielsa* had been becalmed astern of her.

The group which passed south of the Crozet Islands were much better served with wind. During a four hour middle watch when *Neptune* to the north only covered one mile, *Debenhams*, 600 miles to the south of her, recorded a full gale. *Adventure* and *Traite de Rome*, next to the southwards, recorded fresh to strong winds at that time; these two held first and second in handicap position, while third was *Kings Legend*, whose track was also well to the south.

Heath's Condor, under double-reefed main with her ribbon yankee poled out to weather, also reported gale force on 2 November—'a day highlighted by exhilarating fast sailing'. Her track was also well to the south, as was that of *B & B Italia*, whose speed, corrected for handicap allowance, was then only fractionally less than *Kings Legend*.

Passing nearest to the Crozet Islands of this

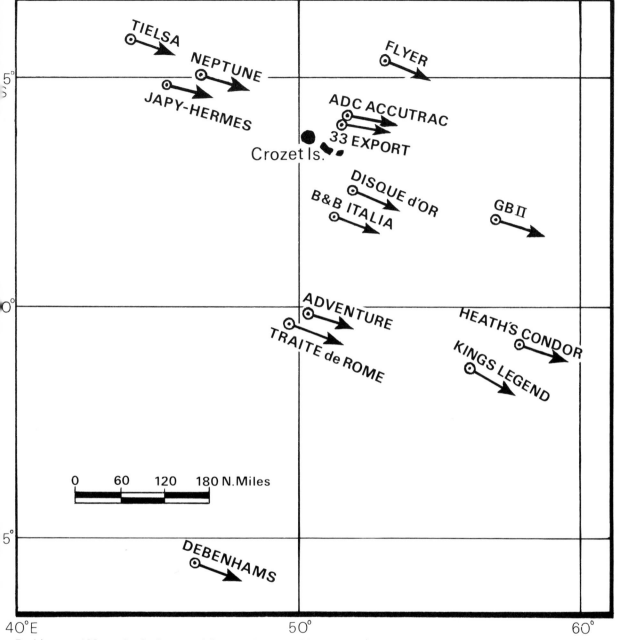

Positions on 4 November in the area of Crozet Island. At this stage those which passed south of the Island were better served with wind than the more northerly group.

southern section of the fleet was *G.B.II*. 'Will the Forties not Roar this year?' Robert James asked, but the truth was that the wind was then roaring vigorously in the Fifties, and he was to have none of it until he got down there;

however, his watch on deck were to put up with a snow squall before then.

Anywhere other than in the Southern Ocean the wind would have seemed ample; indeed the day the first snow squall hit them *GB II* covered

250 miles, but *Heath's Condor* did 20 miles better.

A further 650 miles to the east of Crozet lies another French island; this is Kerguelen or Desolation Island, with magnificent scenery in its 85 mile length from north to south, and many glaciers coming down to the sea on the east and west sides. 'Had a shot of whisky in the coffee to celebrate the passing of Kerguelen', logged *Flyer* on 7 November when 15 miles to the north, 'Wish we had time to visit them'. With a full gale from the north she was surfing very fast under mainsail, blast reacher and forestay sail, as she passed two big killer whales at 50 yards; it was the first time in the race that she had no mizzen hoisted. Visibility was low in driving rain and the sea was confused as the echo sounder showed the depth coming down to 130 metres. Once in deep water again, Gerard Dijkstra, as navigator, relaxed again while *Flyer's* crew settled down in a determined drive to improve their position; she was actually lying in about fourth place on handicap, but all onboard felt they were far behind as they heard on the radio enthusiastic reports of high speeds from the yachts which were well to the south.

ADC Accutrac, 33 Export and *Neptune* also passed northwards of Kerguelen, but they were lagging well behind having met calms and headwinds since Crozet; yet they were a long way ahead of *Gauloises II*, which had been fighting against severe conditions after leaving Port Elizabeth with a replaced rudder. 'Windward sailing very cold in these parts' logged John Tanner in *ADC Accutrac*; when at last her wind turned back to westerly, it was so light that her log re-christened the area the 'Whispering Forties'. She was to experience no more gales until she was south of the forties and into the fifties.

Tielsa and *Japy-Hermes* had passed north of Crozet, but steered southwards of Kerguelen in the track of *Disque D'Or* which was well up the fleet on handicap. She passed fairly close south of the island on 7 November.

Handicap leader at this stage was still *Adventure*, who had experienced a gale when south of the Crozet; snow hurtled at the watch on deck until it gave way to sleet as the wind backed to south-west, but they were sailing the yacht very fast, and correctly felt that *Adventure* was doing very well; she was following a similar track to *Heath's Condor* and also to *Kings Legend*, which had passed south of Kerguelen just 24 hours ahead, and had by then gained second place on handicap from *Traite de Rome*, keeping on a track 60 miles south of *Adventure*. However, at that stage the difference between these three, allowing for handicaps, represented no more than hundredths of a knot. *Kings Legend's* skipper was still unwell and medical advice was requested by radio from the doctor in *Heath's Condor*.

Heath's Condor was very well in the lead on passing about 300 miles south of Kerguelen on 5 November, some 150 miles ahead of *Kings Legend*. The same gale and snow which hit *Adventure* on November 4, caught up with her. 'Bad broach', Robin Knox-Johnston logged when the wind was force 7, 'Handed gale kite, via the ocean, set storm kite'. However, it gave her a record day's run of 270 miles and 1000 miles sailed in four days. Yet even this was not enough, 'We do not seem to be pulling ahead as fast as we would like' logged Robin Knox-Johnston.

G.B.II only reached the Fifties as she approached Kerguelen, and on the run from Crozet lost out to those further south. For her the winds had remained in the westerly sector, but they had not been strong enough for her 77 foot length to catch up on the handicap it carried. On 5 November a passing front gave her a few hours of wind force 6 in snow showers, but Robert James was praying for good steady gales which would drive her at maximum speed without the need for his crew to struggle with her different spinnakers. His prayers for gales were to be answered, but only when they got down to the Fifties. Meantime, on passing to the south of Kerguelen, she was

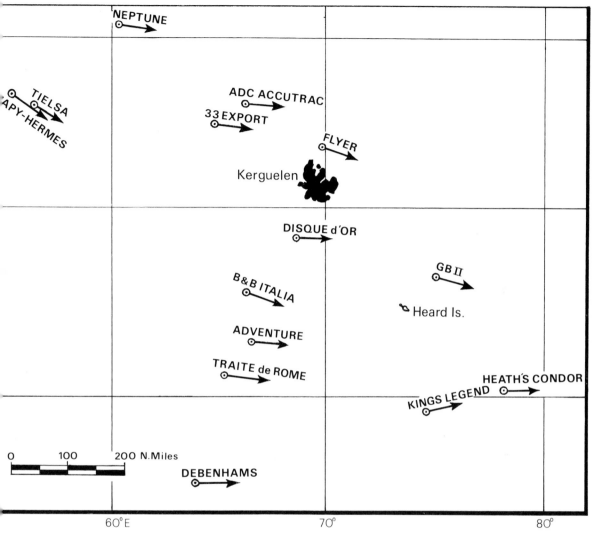

Positions on 7 November in the area of Kerguelen and Heard Islands. At this stage *Adventure* was best placed on handicap, with *Kings Legend* and *Traite de Rome* competing for second position.

lying eleventh on handicap, ahead only of some of the yachts to the north.

Once yachts reached the Fifties, ice became of growing interest as the weather got colder. On 5 November, in 51° south, *Adventure* received a special ice report, based on American satellite photos and passed on to her by radio from Blandford. This gave the line of the pack ice as mainly at 60° south, but in 90° east longitude it stretched north to 57° south. This important message was broadcast to all the fleet.

Debenhams was then on her planned composite great circle course towards 59° south, and her own observations of sea temperature had already suggested that ice lay slightly further north than the normal for the time of year—which would have been up to 59° south thereabouts. Thus immediately on receipt of *Adventure*'s warning message, she turned due east on parallel sailing along 57° south, as she had no wish to invite trouble, particularly at night.

Surely the early explorers, such as Kerguelen-Tremavec who first discovered the island named after him, when feeling his way cautiously among the icy waters would have found it difficult to believe that two centuries later a sailing yacht would be able to call England by radio to find an up-to-date position of the pack ice as seen by a space craft orbiting overhead. He might have been amazed, too, to hear that such a small craft, manned by amateur yachtsmen, would continue to run flat out in a storm, even through the night.

Yet even when the wind reached force 10, storm force, blowing from the north to make the pack ice a lee shore, *Debenhams* sailed on at high speed with the trisail set; a slight coating of ice began to coat the rigging.

After 13 hours of this storm force, the wind eased to a full gale, but the barometer went on dropping to reach the bottom of 972 mm 24 hours later on 7 November. Then, as it rose, there was a superb display of aurora Australis covering the whole sky; *Adventure*, 200 miles to the north, also reported aurora that night, following a day of full gale. 'Vessel rolling heavily. Occasional snow showers', she logged.

Heath's Condor also reported a fabulous aurora display, following a beautiful sunset, although the wind was still gale force. Perhaps almost as beautiful to Robin Knox-Johnston was the sight of the log showing 28 knots as David Alan-Williams held her steady through a surf ride. Also in that gale, with a rough sea and heavy swell, Julian Gildersleeve persuaded the generator back into life.

Onboard *G.B.II*, heating was becoming quite a problem down below as it was so cold that the gas would not vaporise in their heater. John Deane used his motor-bike helmet to keep his head warm, while it could also be useful on deck if pieces of ice fell down from the rigging.

Kings Legend, in 55°S on 10 November, was the first to sight an iceberg. A few hours later *G.B.II*, 120 miles away, made her first iceberg sighting; while at almost the same time *Heath's Condor* sighted one with several growlers to leeward of it. That night, sailing at $10\frac{1}{2}$ knots with a lookout posted in the pulpit, she sailed within two boat's lengths of a growler about the size of a mini-car. She must have passed several other bergs that night unseen, judging by their positions reported by the yachts following in her track.

Debenhams, still easily the furthest south, made her first ice sighting early on 11 November, a day after the leaders, following many days and nights of freezing lookout in the weather rigging, when no-one but Tom Woodfield really believed that they would actually see icebergs, perhaps as they had never seen them before. That day her constant companions were bergs, bergy bits which are lumps of ice about the size of a small cottage, and growlers which are smaller still, often coloured green and barely showing above the water.

So near the magnetic south pole, the compass needle wanted to point nearly downwards, so its lateral directional force was small. This problem was noted by several yachts, but it particularly affected those well to the south. Among these was *Adventure*, whose navigator found that he could get stronger directional force by temporarily removing the corrector magnets, an expedient used by ships in these areas before the era of the gyro compass.

This made it difficult to know where *Debenhams* had been steering and at noon on 11 November she found herself in 58°31′ S, or 91 miles south of her planned parallel sailing. However no concentrations of ice had been seen, and the sea temperature at $-\frac{1}{2}$°C was fractionally higher than three days earlier. Also no birds associated with pack ice, nor any ice blink, had been observed. Thus it was assessed onboard that she might well have passed the bulge northward of Antarctic coastal ice which a week earlier had been observed by satellite, and often occurs in those longitudes.

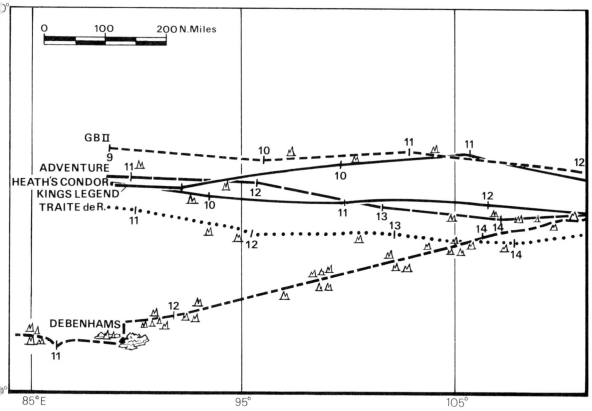

Sailing through the ice in mid November. *Debenhams* found herself actually within the pack ice on 11 November and was forced to turn west of north to clear it.

Many more icebergs were sighted by the yachts than those shown here from the positions logged.

During the evening of 11 November, with darkness lasting about three and a half hours each night, she began to meet rather more pieces of broken ice than were healthy, and here is an account by Tom Woodfield of what followed.

'The vessel had to be conned either from the bows or from the weather shrouds, which proved the best position on all counts. It took the form of "Port 5—Starboard 10—steady", to weave through the brash ice. Soon it became apparent even in the darkness, that much of this ice had its origins in pack ice, the flat topped pieces of broken sea ice, eroded heavily at the waterline, becoming all too frequent obstacles amongst the other loose ice.'

'As we made the decision to turn away northwards, it was snowing as well as dark. We

came upon loose ice, brash and fragmented pack in wind-blown concentrations which barred our way.'

'This was normal for the pack edge—so we had certainly reached our limit south. The golden rules for any vessel near ice is not to commit her to working it unless absolutely necessary; then to hit the lighter pieces and avoid the larger ones when progressing into more difficult and concentrated conditions. Little did I even think that I should even have to apply these rules in a yacht, but soon there was no alternative, and we were forced to proceed north-westerly.'

'John Ridgway handled the craft well; with all hands on deck, the wind blowing at 40 knots, amidst a considerable swell, we tacked and tacked continuously. We sailed in any open water we came across, then on approaching more ice, luffed up to take the way off her, and then gently laid *Debenhams* against the ice. As the sails filled again, she gradually gathered way and eased through the ice to the next parcel of open water.'

'For about three hours we did this, with a great deal of scraping and grinding, besides taking a few hard knocks. Eventually we cleared the ice as daylight returned.'

'With daylight there was a sense of relief in everybody, although ahead still lay innumerable bergs and bits to be avoided, besides the freezing conditions on deck. There was considerable ice blink to the southwards, indicating heavy concentrations of pack ice only a few miles off. If this had been seen the evening before it would have warned us in time to avoid any contact', concluded Tom Woodfield.

Later in Auckland both John and Marie-Christine told me that those few hours of darkness in the ice had made their whole journey from their home in 58° north latitude worthwhile, and not surprisingly several of the crew told of this as the most exciting part of the passage. From the race point of view their course had really only taken *Debenhams* a few miles too far south on a leg of over seven thousand miles; it can only have cost her a few hours in extra time.

On clearing the pack ice *Debenhams* planned a course of due east, to avoid further encounter with the pack ice, but actually she steered well northwards of this due to the poor directive force on the compass so near to the magnetic pole, combined with the helmsmen's natural tendency to steer up and avoid the risk of gybing in strong westerly winds. She still had to pass many bergs, bergy bits and growlers, while one forenoon a day or two later was particularly exciting. 'In hard sailing conditions,' described Tom Woodfield, 'under a cloudless sky behind a cold front, we entered an area where a large berg had recently disinteg-

Even when *Debenhams* got clear of the pack ice, she still had to pass many bergs, such as this one.

rated. The sea was strewn with lumps, all rising and falling dramatically in a large swell; any one of them was sufficient to deal us a death blow had we ventured too close.'

The temperatures when sailing in the Southern Ocean were in the region −2°C to −7°C, but the chill factor from the wind made the effective temperature on a body much colder. Hands and feet were continually numbed, with stiff fingers making work on deck difficult; in some people this effect lasted long after air temperatures had risen; Cornelius van Rietschoten, skipper of *Flyer*, still had numb feet after arrival in Auckland.

None of the yachts iced up, but there were reports of slush on deck as water and spray where shipped, while occasionally a thin coating of ice formed on the rigging. Frozen snow packed on the windward side of anything metal, particularly masts, and this created a hazard as pieces fell from aloft.

Ice was only one of the hazards of the Southern Ocean, and while *Kings Legend* was still among the bergs and literally thousands of miles from any secure harbour, on 11 November she discovered a serious leak aft; a crack opened and closed with the rudder pressure as she surged on the waves in half a gale of wind.

She immediately shortened sail to ease the helm, and turned on a course towards Australia. A close examination suggested that the glass fibre had de-laminated around the rudder post. Once it was established that the pump could easily control the inflow of water, it was decided to press on again for Auckland under full sail, keeping a careful watch on the leak. Other yachts in the area were informed and it was arranged that *Heath's Condor, G.B.II* and *Adventure* would listen out for radio reports every six hours, in case the leak should become worse. Robin Knox-Johnston plotted the course *Heath's Condor* would need to steer back to *Kings Legend* in case of real trouble; if she stopped completely or even sank, it would mean beating some 170 miles to windward, and he noted the sea temperature was barely above

freezing point as he thought what it might be like to spend 24 hours in a rubber raft. It was just this possibility which had made the race committee insist that life rafts must have double bottoms. However, *G.B.II* was some 60 miles closer to *Kings Legend*, while *Adventure* was about two days sailing to windward of her. Probably there was no big ship within hundreds of miles, so this damage report stressed that throughout much of the course the safety of any yacht in real trouble must depend upon her fellow competitors and reliable radio communications.

After two days, *Kings Legend* logged 'Leak under full control—no worse yet', just after she had altered course to avoid a medium sized berg. She was to continue the 6 hour radio check for another week.

Meantime one of her potential rescuers had a life and death problem of her own, following a terrific day of near gale with a record run of 298 miles on 12 November. 'Surely you can scratch a couple more miles out of the chart to make it 300?' suggested most of the crew, but to Robin navigation meant precision and not just figures that looked nice. The following day the wind was down to force 4 and conditions looked quiet while a gas bottle was changed, the heavy spinnaker was set, and some running rigging replaced. Then suddenly the lazy spinnaker filled and its sheet caught Bill Abram, to lift him over the guard wire into the sea with the yacht sailing at 10 knots.

Fortunately most of the crew was still on deck, so there was no delay in throwing a lifebuoy, letting go the spinnaker and starting the main engine: but the folding propeller jammed shut. The spinnaker was reluctant to come down as it pressed against the mast and rigging, so the yacht at first refused to come round. Fortunately Bill had caught hold of the lifebuoy in the water, and fine seamanship by Peter Blake, at the wheel, brought the yacht alongside him after 10 minutes in the water, a few seconds later Dr. Dickson was binding up his injured hand and thawing him out after his swim amongst the icebergs. David Alan-Williams also needed attention, as he had been slightly injured when letting the spinnaker fly.

Bill Adam had been wearing a safety harness when thrown overboard, but was not clipped on at that moment. The opinion onboard was that this was fortunate, as had he been checked by the harness the wire guy might have injured him far more severely.

There was still a problem to solve, as the jammed propeller had opened to catch a rope round it, and this could not be cleared from on deck. With the sea too cold to ask any of his crew to dive under the yacht, Robin Knox-Johnston did it himself, and later described that the shock of diving into the water at 1.0°C temperature was like hitting a brick wall, and he lost all feeling in his hand before he had cut through the rope with his knife.

The medical services of David Dickson in *Heath's Condor* were again called upon that day, when *G.B.II* radioed for advice from 180 miles astern.

While changing spinnakers, as light winds were turning into a heavy blow, a guy caught round the waist of Nick Dunlop and squeezed him severely when the full weight of the spinnaker dragging in the sea came on it. The guy was promptly cut, and the spinnaker lost, but it was a very near thing from a fatal accident; Nick was quite seriously injured although, with careful attention onboard and medical advice by radio, he suffered no lasting harm. Robert James had also been slightly injured but was not in any way disabled.

These 13 November accidents in *Heath's Condor* and *G.B.II* both came when the weather was working up for the biggest depression to pass over the fleet throughout the leg from Cape Town to Auckland. Its centre probably passed fairly close to the south of *Debenhams* whose barometer dropped to 965 mm. It brought gales to all the southern group, and drove then fast, in spite of several incidents. This in force 8 winds *ADC Accutrac* was pooped for the first time 'fair and square'

as she ran 46 miles in a four-hour watch with two reefs in her mainsail and a poled out jib. 'Good for us to have strong winds—suits the boat' she logged.

At about the same time *Adventure* reported a spectacular broach in force 8. 'The storm spinnaker pole broke at the downhaul as the vessel broached to. The main was aback, held by the preventer, and the vessel was dragged sideways in heavy seas'. The spinnaker was recovered intact, but its sheet and guy were lost.

Some 300 miles north of *Adventure*, there were strong winds for *33 Export* in 50° S, and she added to the 13 November accidents when her main boom broke. Sailing on at reduced speed under an improvised rig, her crew set to work on repairs, and considering the lack of tools and shortage of suitable material, they achieved an amazingly resourceful feat of seamanship. With only a hacksaw blade they cut out a section some 15 by 8 inches from the thick aluminium bulkhead door which separated the forward part of the yacht from the main cabin; then they shaped and bolted this to the main boom. It was thoroughly well tested soon afterwards when 19 November *33 Export* made her best day's run of 261 miles, steering before a westerly gale. On handicap she still lay in the second half of the fleet, as she had lost out by keeping in the northerly group. (See page 159.)

Even *Neptune* in 49°S, some 800 miles north of *Debenhams*, reported strong winds from the west giving her a day's run on 13 November of 261 miles, which was to be her best of the race up to Auckland. *Japy-Hermes* covered just the same distance that day, keeping approximately to the 51st parallel; during the passage of this depression none of the fleet could complain of wind shortage.

B & B Italia, running along about the same parallel as *Adventure* and some 60 miles astern of her, also suffered gale damage. The first report was that she had lost her forestay and a spreader, so was heading for Hobart under jury rig. However, her crew did marvels aloft, especially considering the weather conditions, and a day or so later Corrado Di Majo, perhaps strengthened by his experiences in the Single-handed Trans-atlantic race, reported by radio that he was continuing on his course for Auckland.

Starved of strong winds earlier on, when she was keeping in the Forties, *Flyer* really came into her own, recording fine runs day after day following up her best of 281 miles on 13 November. She was just north of the iceberg limit but well placed for wind.

'*Kings Legend* is 267 miles ahead,' Flyer logged that day, 'and even if she has to slow down a lot it will be difficult to catch her. Anyhow we wish her the best of luck'. Indeed the leak seemed to have slowed down *Kings Legend*, as in the week which followed that comment she sailed about 200 miles less than *Flyer*'s 1,768 miles, an amazing run for a yacht of 65 ft. length and close enough to the best week by *Heath's Condor* of 1,801 miles. She was certainly being pushed hard by Cornelius

van Rietschoten, who throughout those days insisted on as much sail as possible, even if the yacht broached frequently. The helmsmen found it difficult in a big sea with white crests to keep on course with spinnaker set 'We try hard to be kind for the spinnaker and keep broaching to a minimum'. Next day with a big irregular swell 15 feet high and some very gusty winds, the main boom broke just aft of the preventer tackle during a broach. The mainsail was undamaged, the big spinnaker lowered with difficulty, and she sailed on without loss of speed under blast reacher, genoa staysail and mizzen. Her broken main boom was repaired in 10 hours, and after that hectic downwind dash she could log 'Everything onboard in working order again although the toe rail track is missing (used for repair of main boom)'.

Before the end of this super-fast week the leaders had begun to edge northwards on the great circle track for Cape North. Boats could pass either side of New Zealand, and there had been much discussion of the relative merits of

Flyer really came into her own recording fine runs day after day, following a shortage of strong winds earlier in

the leg. Here her speed can be read as just under 15 knots, as the main boom drags through the sea.

going north-about or south-about. Coming up from a track well south, the difference in distance represents no more than a day becalmed on one side of the islands or another. Generally the north-about route was considered likely to suffer less calms, as it runs for a much shorter distance to leeward of high land in New Zealand; however, it was expected that any skipper who was not too well placed might take a gamble of catching up by going south-about. None did, partly because none except *Gauloises II* had really been left behind; however, some suggested that eagerness to get away from sailing in the Antarctic cold was also a factor, as a south-about track would have meant at least another day before turning northwards for New Zealand.

Heath's Condor, in the lead, kept to her parallel sailing until on 15 November she was in 135° E longitude; then she turned north-easterly to the great circle course; this gave her fast reaching conditions as a change from running. Two days later she was 400 miles south of Hobart, and Peter Blake, as a New Zealander, told how they might expect rougher conditions in the Tasman Sea than anything they had experienced in an unusually moderate run through the Southern Ocean. Certainly a gale from the south-east suggested something of the sort as they reached the latitude of New Zealand's southern point; they were also welcomed to the Tasman by a very large Fin whale. The wind soon eased to moderate or fresh, and later fell light as they watched 'a magnificent display of effortless power by a wandering albatross'. They felt thwarted as

Even under spinnaker, with the wind well abaft the beam, there was ample spray over the deck of *Flyer* in a Southern Ocean blow.

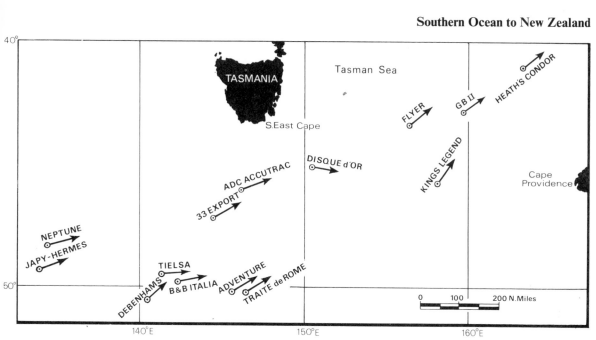

Positions on 21 November with the leaders well up the Tasman Sea.

they heard how the yachts astern were catching up fast. *G.B.II* was 210 miles behind, after sailing 80 miles further that day. The wind soon came again for *Heath's Condor*, reaching gale force from the westwards when half way up the Tasman Sea; but again it dropped very light before she sighted Cape Reinga lighthouse on 24 November.

The fleet was well spread astern of the two maxi-yachts; by this time the northern group was getting the best of things to make up for the advantage in stronger winds which the southern group had enjoyed in the first half of the race, and also for the extra distance the northern group had to sail. In the three days 19, 20 and 21 November, two northerly yachts *ADC Accutrac* and *33 Export* logged 710 and 700 miles respectively, while a couple of hundred miles to the south, *Adventure* and *Traite de Rome*, covered only 590 and 564 miles. At the end of those three days, the northern pair was a good deal closer to Cape Reinga, and *Adventure* had dropped well back in the fleet handicap order after leading for much of the race. *Flyer* was actually closer to Cape Reinga than *Kings Legend*, and these two

at that time looked as though once again they would be competing for leg winner.

33 Export, ADC Accutrac and also *Disque D'Or* continued to hold good winds, both keeping to well above 200 miles for each of the days to follow until they sighted Cape Reinga; 'surfing swell', logged *ADC Accutrac* when 25 November gave her best day's run of the leg, 'only a few broaches'.

Meantime the Tasman Sea treated *Adventure, Traite de Rome* and *Debenhams* of the southern group to gales alternating with calms. 'The wind diminished more quickly than the sea, prohibiting the use of the spinnaker' logged *Adventure*, following a day on which a westerly gale which ripped the mainsail. *Traite de Rome* on 24 November reported all her spinnakers blown out, putting her speed down a whole knot. *Debenhams* logged a strong gale, force 9, on 23 November, yet three days later it was not more than force 0/1 for hours on end, with a dismal day's run of 76 miles. There was no need to remind Tom Woodfield, her navigator, of his pre-race advice that the winds were usually steadier in the Fifties, even if stronger than in the Roaring Forties.

83

Kings Legend had got ahead of *Flyer* again, as on 25 November she stood four miles north of Cape Reinga to avoid a lee under the land; *Flyer* passed close to the headland about three hours later. There was still some 200 miles to Auckland, coasting New Zealand's North Island, but a high pressure area was approaching from Tasmania, so anything might happen. 'We need some luck to reduce our distance from K.L.' logged *Flyer*, and the intensive struggle in dying winds for the line at Cape Town was to be the story again.

At about that time *Heath's Condor* was beating up Rangitot Channel towards the finish line accompanied by a rapidly expanding spectator fleet. From early that morning cars had been converging on the roads that skirt Auckland harbour's north and south shores until they packed solid, with a vast crowd determined to see the leading yacht cross the line. Peter Montgomery, in Auckland, had

been transmitting lively coverage of the race on the radio, while Peter Blake, onboard *Heath's Condor*, had been interviewed by radio while far out at sea. The people of Auckland seem all to be sailors of one sort or another, and for them the race round the world was one of the great sporting events of the year.

It was 9.33 a.m. local time when *Heath's Condor* crossed the finishing line off Orakei Wharf, and seldom can any yacht have received such a rousing welcome.

Customs and Health Authorities boarded her from their boats, accompanied by Admiral Steiner, the race Chairman, who had been waiting at sea in the committee boat all night.

Then to Marsdon Wharf, in the centre of Auckland's busy international port, and there another great welcome awaited her, followed by an arm-load of champagne from the ever generous race sponsor.

Only 30 days and 9 hours was indeed a

Heath's Condor gets a great reception at Marsden Wharf after winning line honours on the leg to Auckland.

(Right) *Kings Legend* crept into Auckland Harbour two minutes ahead of *Flyer*, to revenge *Flyer*'s close win over her at Cape Town.

superb passage from Cape Town to Auckland, and gave line honours to an impressively fine yacht, which was still too new to have completely polished her tuning, especially as a new mast had been shipped during the first leg of the race.

In the early hours of the next morning, $31\frac{1}{2}$ hours behind her, followed *G.B.II* with another very fine passage. By that time no-one could consider that her crew was partly novice, as they had been when the race started from England. By Auckland they were all seasoned sailors, who had sailed their boat further than many experienced yachtsman sails in a lifetime, and they had come through many more gales too. Certainly *G.B.II* had no teething problems to deal with, indeed during that leg of the race she completed her first 100,000 miles of sailing; but the pangs of so much use by her mast at least balanced the trials of novelty in the mast of *Heath's Condor*.

Yet neither had saved enough time to win the race on handicap, and it seemed likely enough it would be *Kings Legend* or *Flyer* as they rounded North Cape to turn southwards, beating along the coast into a moderate breeze, which for a time increased enough to blow out a sail.

Through the night neither knew the position of the other, and pilotage needed careful attention among the off lying islands. Then just as the loom of Auckland's lights came in sight from *Flyer*'s deck, the wind eased. The last of the night breeze carried her into Auckland harbour, and there in the dawn light was *Kings Legend*. She had finished just 1 hour and 15 minutes before, to revenge *Flyer*'s win on the first leg.

Taking the two legs together, after racing half way round the world, there was only 47 minutes between them. 'No major gear breakage—no crew injuries at all—crew and boat in good shape' logged *Flyer*.

The high pressure area coming in from the Tasman would bring a strong probability of light winds down the coast from Cape North,

so it scarcely seemed likely that any of the following yachts could beat these two. Yet *33 Export* had a handicap allowance of over 67 hours from *Kings Legend* and she had made really good use of fresh winds all the way up the Tasman Sea.

Throughout the whole leg her running mate had been *ADC Accutrac*, and with their northerly track they had sailed some 200 miles further than the southern group. They reached North Cape only ten hours apart, but *33 Export* gained a couple of hours during the beat down the east coast of New Zealand, to finish only eight hours behind. *33 Export* was one of the smaller yachts and also had the benefit of a 5.6% age allowance, so on handicap she bettered *ADC Accutrac* by two days. Better still, her handicap put her $8\frac{1}{2}$ hours ahead of *Kings Legend* to the leading position for the leg.

The enthusiasm and excitement of *33 Export*'s crew delighted everyone as she came into Marsden Wharf, perhaps the more so as the yacht herself was showing ample signs of her age. They were to have an anxious wait to know whether *Traite de Rome* or possibly *Adventure* would snatch the lead from them, just as they had snatched it from *Kings Legend*.

Traite de Rome still had 18 hours to beat *33 Export* and no-one in Auckland knew precisely where she was. Since taking over from *Adventure* many days before, she had held best place on handicap coming up through the Roaring Forties from further south; then on 24 November she reported all her spinnakers blown out, so after that her progress was uncertain. However, she was somewhere near North Cape, fighting it out, boat for boat, with *Adventure*, who had been her running mate throughout the leg.

There still appeared an outside chance that she might snatch the victory from *33 Export*, and one or two unconfirmed reports from up the coast put her closer than she really was. The high pressure area had moved over her, so that winds were light; indeed *Adventure* and she were becalmed for a time only 90 miles short of the finish, and then made quiet progress down the coast.

As though 34 days hard racing from Cape Town was not enough, the crew of *33 Export* sailed out to meet them and duly cheered in *Adventure*. By then *33 Export* was assured of her win for the leg by some eight hours, so her crew could cheer all the more enthusiastically as 23 minutes later *Traite de Rome* crept across

the line for a well earned second place, beating *Kings Legend* into third by 36 minutes.

The crew of *33 Export* had good reason to be more excited than ever as they went back into Marsden Wharf the victors.

33 Export about to cross the line at Auckland Harbour. She was to prove the winner of the leg from Cape Town— one of the smallest yachts in the race and also one of the oldest.

New Zealand and the Race

By His Excellency the Governor General of New Zealand
Sir Keith Holyoake G.C.M.G., CH.

New Zealand is a maritime country, so it gave us great pleasure to be host to the deep sea sailors from many countries competing in the Whitbread Round the World Race.

I particularly enjoyed meeting them, men and women, when at the Royal New Zealand Yacht Squadron I presented the prizes won for the stage of the race from Cape Town to Auckland. I heard stirring tales of adventure at sea, sailing among icebergs in full gales. Also I heard how so many had taken the opportunity of their stopover in Auckland to visit many parts of New Zealand; it was pleasing to note the enthusiastic impressions of our country among young people coming from so many other countries. Clearly New Zealanders had given them the warm welcome they deserved.

We admire their courage and fortitude, while the lively spirit in the fleet of yachts was a fine example of the brotherhood of the sea. It was heart warming to see how a floating community, of which the members were mostly strangers to each other before the start of the race in England, had become firm friends with a common purpose by the time they set off from New Zealand to sail on around Cape Horn.

'New Zealand is a maritime country'.

A Kiwi Competitor's Plea

The rules read 'Cape Horn to Port'. Ever since my early yachting days racing a P class with the Takepuna boating club one of my aims has been to round Cape Horn under sail. It has taken me over 100,000 miles of ocean racing and cruising to achieve, but what a highlight! After the frustrations of the first leg of the 77/78 Whitbread Round the World Race from Portsmouth to Cape Town, the speeds and severe cold of the run to Auckland, the intensity and sheer pleasure of the New Zealand hospitality, and then the icebergs, hail and snow of 63 degrees south in the Southern Pacific Ocean, to approach and round Cape Horn under full sail aboard the 77 foot sloop *Heath's Condor* meant a great deal to me, seeming to justify everything.

The Royal Naval Sailing Association, which set up this race, talks about running another Round the World in 1981. We *must* have an entry of New Zealand design and construction, crewed solely by Kiwis. The time to begin such a project is now. Let's show the rest of the world what we really can do in the longest and toughest ocean race in the world.

Peter Blake

Peter Blake steers *Heath's Condor* running before a big Southern Ocean sea.

7 Over Christmas in Auckland

Each yacht, whatever the time of day or night, was timed across the finish line off Orakei Wharf by Tony Yates of the Royal New Zealand Yacht Squadron, and she was led to her berth by a committee boat representing the Squadron. Indeed the Royal New Zealand Yacht Squadron was the host club for the stay in Auckland; as well as handling the finishing arrangements, it also organised the start of the next leg to Rio and this included scrutineering.

Crews were at all times welcomed to the Squadron club house, often in person by Hugh Littler, the Commodore, and also by Douglas Dick, the Secretary Manager, who had scarcely drawn a breath since the Squadron had handled the One Ton world championships shortly beforehand. The club house is beside Auckland Harbour's fine bridge, and some two miles from the centre of the city, so the berthing area, reserved entirely for competing yachts by the Auckland Harbour Board, was Marsden Wharf, near the central Downtown section of the city and just off the bottom of Queen Street, Auckland's principal shopping centre. It was also close to the impressive office of the Harbour Board where the skippers were formally entertained, and from which Harry Julian, as deputy chairman of the Board and also a member of the Squadron's race committee, could keep a helpful eye on things.

Practically spending his whole days and nights at the wharf was Warwick Walker, a member of the Squadron and also a representative of Whitbreads, the sponsors, on whose behalf he had the pleasant task of presenting each yacht on arrival with pre-cooled champagne to toast their achievement, and also enough beer to allay their thirst; to some, the packet of waiting mail he gave to each was even more important. Warwick was in constant demand to advise on a whole host of problems, ranging from repair facilities to hotel accommodation, and from local pilotage to the best way of sightseeing in South Island.

Also frequently at the wharf and onboard the yachts was Bob Stanton, Rear Commodore of the Squadron and chairman of its special committee for the race. This was acting partly on behalf of, and partly in conjunction with, the main R.N.S.A. race committee, which was itself represented in Auckland by Admiral Otto Steiner, his vice-chairman Captain Hans Hamilton and Erroll Bruce. For the three of us from England it was a thoroughly enjoyable but extremely busy time. Admiral Steiner maintained his tradition of being first to board each yacht, while we were constantly on call throughout the time in Auckland, often onboard yachts at Marsden Wharf, at the repair yards or even while tuning at sea; also we regularly attended meetings or entertainments at the Squadron club-house. Otherwise we were in our hotel room office near the wharf, where a steady stream of yachtsmen came to see us, some to raise race points, others to discuss matters about their own yachts, and the ladies, particularly, to borrow our adjoining bathrooms while we were engaged in our daily

(Left) Bob Stanton, chairman of the New Zealand race committee, and Mrs Stanton talk to David Leslie, *Adventure*'s skipper, and (right) Warwick Walker dis-cusses matters with Robin Knox-Johnston, *Heath's Condor*'s skipper.

(Below) Marsden wharf normally had a crowd of interested onlookers, while it was highly convenient to the city for the yacht crews.

breakfast time conference; this was usually joined by Raymond Seymour, Deputy Chairman of Whitbreads, or other members of his firm when visiting from England.

All the competing yachts were adopted by various hospitable families who helped those onboard to make the most of their visit to New Zealand. There was also a full programme of social activities, including formal receptions for all the crews by the Squadron and the Mayor of Auckland, besides less formal parties in plenty.

The crews inevitably had a great deal of work for their yachts, so particularly valuable was a large cargo shed on Marsden Wharf where sails could be laid out for repair, unstepped masts could be attended to, gear sorted and provisions organised.

So long as other competitors were at sea, those in harbour were monitoring their progress with the keenest of interest. It was not just a matter of watching whether lower handicap late comers could better any one of them already in; more, it was that each crew formed a part of the race community; they knew each other as much through the inter-yacht radio network as through actual meeting ashore, so it was natural to keep this contact going between those at sea and those in harbour. Indeed the most up-to-date information about likely arrivals always came from the fleet itself.

Thus even when the handicap win by *33 Export* was certain after the arrival of *Adventure* and *Traite de Rome*, keen interest was kept up on the trio of *Tielsa, Neptune* and *Japy Hermes* as they approached North Cape. Onboard *Flyer* at Marsden Wharf, an extremely accurate forecast was given about the arrival time of their fellow Dutchman *Tielsa*; it was almost as though they knew in advance exactly what tacks Dirk Nauta would take when beating to windward up the coast.

Next were the French pair *Japy-Hermes* and *Neptune*. Here there were different views among the crew of French *33 Export* about which of the pair would arrive first. *Japy-Hermes*

seemed just in the lead approaching North Cape, but some were confident that Bernard Deguy in *Neptune* would make up for this in light windward work down the coast. They proved right, and *Neptune* sailed in nearly 7 hours before *Japy-Hermes*, whose skipper Jimmy Viant was joined in Auckland by his father, Commodore of the French Union Nationale de Course au Large.

Several other parents and friends of competing crews had flow out to Auckland from their home countries to join in the fun, and already Diana Bonham, mother of Eve in *ADC Accutrac*, had endeared herself to all the fleet by providing a ferry boat to run between Marsden Wharf and the Squadron.

Tielsa sailed into Auckland 37 days out of Cape Town.

With 12 yachts home, representing more than 70% of those continuing on the next leg, the race rules required that its starting date be fixed, but many factors had to be taken into account by the race committee in making this decision.

The ample facilities in Auckland for slipping large yachts had already come into the race planning, but the amount of work needed out of the water could only be assessed when most of the fleet had arrived. Generally the weather on the race from Cape Town had been more moderate than expected, but the pace had been faster and such high speed sailing had led to many problems that needed attention in Auckland.

With the enormous strains when running at very high speeds, the skeg of *Disque D'Or* was strengthened by additional layers of glass fibre.

land. A yacht suddenly accelerating from 10 to perhaps 25 knots, even if surfing only for a few seconds at a time, must put fantastic strains on her skeg and rudder; the wave she rides on may be travelling across the ocean at about the same speed as her surf-ride, yet the water in it, through which she is being forced, is practically stationary.

The effect of these exceptional strains had become apparent halfway through the leg with the report from *Kings Legend* of her leak; so representatives of her builders in Finland flew out to examine her. Then in harbour it was disclosed that several others had similar defects; some of the glass-fibre yachts were strengthened with additional layers of glass-fibre, while aluminium yachts were strengthened by welding. All this needed a good deal of 'slipping time'.

Yacht repairs were not the only factor. Even more important in such a race, with Cape Horn still to come, were people. Only Jean Bernard of *Japy-Hermes* needed hospital treatment, and his appendix was quickly removed; but once the excitement of arrival died down, it was clear that in some cases the human strain had been heavy, partially from living in such close quarters day after day, and especially when yachts had driven on at high speed through storm, fog and ice bergs. In addition there had often been a severe load on skippers for months before the race even started, with practically no relaxation from the worries of organising their entries—problems such as raising enough cash and suitable crews, preparing or even building the yacht in time, providing equipment and provisions, measuring for handicap rating, besides maintaining the right impression on official occasions, in press interviews and on television.

We felt that the stop in Auckland should aim at allowing enough time for each of the crews to be able to spare at least a week completely away from yacht anxieties. New Zealand was perfect for this with its friendly and hospitable people; it also had so much of interest to see and such beautiful scenery to help relaxation. Several reached South Island, either by plane or motor caravan; others went north, for instance to visit the historic treaty house at Waitangi, where in 1832 the Maori and European peoples of New Zealand were formally united under the Queen's Sovereignty. Many more visited the hot springs around Rotorua, and learnt the correct New Zealand pronunciation of geysers.

The 70 % rule for deciding on the start of the next leg was planned with the idea that any yacht seriously held up would have to take her chance about being ready in time, so as not to delay the rest of the fleet. Yet all those already finished seemed to feel that *Gauloises II*, forced to put back into South Africa when her rudder broke off, was a special case, in that she had then got into an entirely different weather pattern and was fighting her way through the Southern Ocean in conditions much more severe than the rest of the fleet. She was bound

to be last in that second leg, but deserved ample time in Auckland to have a fair chance in the following leg. Among those who supported special consideration for her was the skipper of Dutch *Flyer* and this may even have helped *Gauloises II* to be the only yacht to beat *Flyer* on that leg when they reached Rio.

All these factors supported extending the stay in Auckland for a few days beyond the maximum planned. Against this was the problem that in New Zealand the summer holidays start just before Christmas, so many shops and offices would be closed from 23 December. A post-Christmas start would therefore mean that yachts would have to complete Customs and Immigration clearance, embark final stores and last minute provisions, all before Christmas eve; it would also impose an extra burden on the Royal New Zealand Yacht Squadron to handle the start after many of the members would normally have set off on their

B & B Italia (I5555) just ahead of *Debenhams* (K1218) stem comes up to the line. It was little more than a boat's length apart after 7,400 miles of tough racing.

own offshore race. The Squadron's race committee made quite clear that they were prepared to do this, but pointed out that thousands of yachtsmen who would dearly like to see such an important start off Auckland would normally leave in their own yachts on Christmas eve for cruises up the coast.

The R.N.S.A. race committee and the Squadron race committee met jointly, and the unanimous decision was that the next leg would start at 11 a.m. local time on the day after Christmas; the Squadron's own offshore race would start half an hour later, while the Royal Akarana joined in co-operation by timing their offshore race also to start after this. The Customs authority warned of the problems, but agreed to give all possible help, while the police advised that even if most of the local cruising craft had normally left Auckland harbour before Christmas day, there would on this occasion be a very large spectator fleet.

When the fleet had been informed of this decision, the centre of interest shifted to *Debenhams* and *B & B Italia*, beating down the coast almost together. *Debenhams* extreme southerly course had not paid off too well when John Ridgway was forced to beat back through leads in the pack ice, while Corrado di Majo had diverted towards Hobart until temporary repairs to his damaged rigging allowed him to turn *B & B Italia* for Auckland again.

Both these yachts had almost the same handicap rating; it was some 16 feet less than the first yacht home, so a spread of eight days showed surprisingly close racing over such a course. Certainly a good number of craft set out to watch them sail in down Rangitoto Channel. *Debenhams'* tack off the first of the channel buoys took her a few lengths ahead, but John Ridgway is more the adventurer than the close-tacking competitive yachtsman, so he did not cover his fellow competitor. Yachtsmen with local knowledge kept up a vigorous commentary as first one and then the other turned to winning or losing tacks, 'Debs

got her', was the excited cry as *Debenhams* again crossed ahead on port before her final tack; but *B & B Italia* judged it better, and it was her stem that crossed the line first with the two yachts almost overlapping. However, *Debenhams* rated 0.2 feet less, the equivalent of about an hour and a half for the whole leg, so each was a winner in this particular duel.

Only *Gauloises II* then remained at sea, set back by the loss of her rudder and her return to South Africa for replacement. When the rest of the fleet was knocked about by gales on 13 November, she was 1,800 miles behind *Heath's Condor*, so it was quite a different depression which gave her a gale that day, after her barometer had fallen to 986 mm. It was certainly another one, perhaps passing directly over her, which gave a gale from the north-north east on 15 November; this turned fairly rapidly to north-north-west, then the gale backed to west as the barometer began to rise. Eight hours later it reached storm force, still from the west. In terrible seas, she was knocked down and the boat half-filled with water.

Still the storm increased—up to 75 knots and even more. Again she was knocked down and water poured in. She was under bare poles and the seas were mountainous, with the storm blowing unaltered in direction for 24 hours. It was still up to 60 knots—violent storm—when rapidly it fell right away to a moderate breeze from the west-south-west, leaving huge seas to shake the wind out of the heavy jib which was then hoisted. The seas were still big when after a further 12 hours the wind disappeared altogether, with the barometer falling fast again.

Then the wind struck once more from east-north-east and steadily increased to yet another gale on 18 November. It moderated as the barometer continued to fall, then backed to north-west and increased to gale once more as the barometer bottomed at 990 mm.

Four days later, when she was in 50° S, another fierce easterly wind hit her, blowing at 30 knots with a steady high barometer; then it increased to gale force from the north-east as

French crews crowded *Japy-Hermes* to welcome in *Gauloises II* (F 4279).

the barometer dropped, and persisted for 16 hours at gale force from the north.

As she moved north-eastwards in the Roaring Forties on 1 December the ghoster came down with a rush as the lightest of northerly breezes gave way to yet another easterly gale which blew all day, and next day blew even harder from the north-north-east.

Perhaps the voyage of *Gauloises II* was more typical of the Roaring Forties and Screaming Fifties than the much more moderate experiences of all the rest of the fleet. She certainly came through more testing conditions, and as she approached Auckland a week behind any other yacht, those in harbour appreciated their comparatively good fortune and prepared a very warm welcome.

The crew of *Gauloises II* looked surprised when so many craft gathered round her a mile or two short of the finish. Every other French-

man in the race, and many friends too, seemed to be aboard *33 Export* as she set a spinnaker in close escort; several New Zealand craft also joined the escort to honour a crew whose seamanship had gained the admiration of all.

A day or two later came the prize-giving for that leg. The high formality appropriate to the presence of His Excellency the Governor General of New Zealand was skilfully mingled by the Squadron with the very proper *joie-de-vivre* of successful crews—and everyone who had sailed that far in the race had ample reason to feel successful; even the longest-haired male coiffeur remained under reasonable control. Sir Keith Holyoake showed a lively understanding of what made people sail round the world in craft so small, and he also offered to write an introduction for the New Zealand section of this book.

The full results gave food for much discussion and thought. Everyone talked about the advantages of the different routes; the winner and 4th yacht had taken relatively northerly routes, going to about 51°S, while 2nd and 3rd went to about 56°S on southerly routes. So the route did not appear to be a winning factor.

That the first two yachts were among the three lowest rating yachts appeared significant; yet third and fourth were amongst the high rating yachts, and under ten hours covered these four on corrected time. A point frequently mentioned was that every yacht had sailed less than her handicap distance, and this had given an advantage to the low rating yachts. Indeed this was so, as the handicap distance had been previously assessed by the race committee on what it considered a prudent course, and the tracks in the previous Whitbread race were given full weight. Yet in this race yachts had steered much farther south, and this reduced the distance. Perhaps the crew of *Gauloises II* may have wondered at times whether so southerly a course was indeed prudent navigation as storm after storm struck her, often with headwinds.

However, a navigator who had sailed the longer more northerly course with success made some calculations; had the handicap distance been assessed as low as 6,800 miles, instead of 7,400, *33 Export* would still have been the winner, and the order throughout would have been unchanged. It was clear that at least in leg 2, under the particular circumstances encountered, the maxi-yachts would have had to sail at a fantastic speed to win. Thus *G.B.II* would have needed to complete the course in 27 days, averaging 264 miles each day, a distance she only achieved on three days in the leg.

Another keen navigator tested the suggestion that the handicap should be calculated on the time taken instead of the distance. The time-on-time system is frequently used in shorter offshore races, so that the faster the race the less handicap benefit goes to the low rating boats. This leg was a fast race with practically no windward work, and he showed that under this system the winner might have been *Kings Legend*. Yet the same system had to be used throughout the race round the world, and ample windward work could be expected in the race as a whole, so the time-on-distance system had been selected as most suitable for this race.

Eric Tabarly, well before the start in England, had announced his plan to join the race at Auckland in his *Pen Duick VI*, and this had been discussed by the full race committee. The International Offshore Rule had been changed in 1975 to forbid a rating certificate to any yacht whose keel had a specific gravity greater than lead. *Pen Duick*'s keel included spent uranium, much heavier than lead; yet we were keen to let yacht and skipper race, as both had done so in the first Whitbread Round the World race, and the new rule had come in after the date when we had announced the general conditions for this present race. We also felt that the other yachts would like to test their performance against her well known ability. Thus her entry had been accepted, subject to all the detailed requirements of the race, and these included a valid rating certificate.

Immediately *Pen Duick* secured at Marsden Wharf a representative of the race committee boarded her, and handed to Eric Tabarly another copy of the detailed communication instructions for the race, as the worldwide change of international radio frequencies on 1 January 1978 would almost certainly mean that *Pen Duick* would need different crystals. Eric Tabarly then showed a photo copy of his rating certificate and pointed his finger to its expiry date of 30 November 1977; he felt that it was in date as the race had started on 27 August at Portsmouth. Certainly we were very pleased to see Eric, and discussed with him how well *Gauloises II*, also owned by him, had performed in weather much more severe than the other yachts had met.

Meantime it had been suggested to the race committee that as the international rating of *Heath's Condor* had included a factor for the special material of her original mast, it would only be fair for *Pen Duick* to carry a similar handicap factor for her uranium keel. This seemed quite reasonable except that as our race rules had ordained that it be handicapped under the International Offshore Rules we felt unauthorised to make arbitrary changes to these. We therefore ruled that *Pen Duick VI* should be handicapped according to her international rating certificate.

This led *Heath's Condor* to protest against the race committee's decision—a protest is a perfectly proper and sportsmanlike means by which any yacht can require decisions to be examined by an independent body—and Leslie Williams appreciated that there was room for doubt. The Royal New Zealand Yacht Squadron formally heard the case, with a jury of thoroughly experienced international yachtsmen. This found that there was no means of imparting a penalty on *Pen Duick VI* under the race rules; her entry must be subject to a valid rating certificate, but she could be accepted provisionally while this was being checked. The validity of this certificate was a problem which we felt could only be decided by the international offshore body, and this could not be done before the start. Eric Tabarly was himself away from New Zealand until just before the start, so on his return Bob Stanton, chairman of the Squadron committee, accom-

Crews as well as yachts needed attention before the leg around Cape Horn.

panied by one of the R.N.S.A. race committee, went onboard *Pen Duick*, where the position was explained to Eric. He seemed quite content that she be allowed to enter the race provisionally, although the decision as to whether she was entitled to win any prizes could not be made until later. Should the decision go against eligibility, then her entry could not be confirmed; there was no question that disqualification could arise, as a yacht not entered cannot possibly be disqualified.

All this seemed to be understood and Eric smiled as though he was keen to get on with the sailing and not too concerned with the paperwork. We were very relieved that this great ocean racer should be so tolerant of a situation which must surely have upset a lesser man than

Traite de Rome (left) and *Adventure* secured beside her, had duelled with each other on similar tracks all the way from Cape Town, to reach Auckland only 23 minutes apart. *Traite de Rome* had the lowest handicap rating of all, with *Adventure* rating next to her.

Eric, for whom the racing seems more important than the prizes.

Christmas was a Sunday, so the holiday began on Friday afternoon. Thus the yachts needed to be stored and provisioned, with Custom, Immigration and race formalities completed, three days before the start on Monday. This was a problem in some ways, but it also allowed a relaxed Christmas in harbour before setting off on another thoroughly demanding leg of the course.

Several crews had their own parties on Christmas Eve, aboard their yachts or ashore. It was indeed a truly happy yacht party which I was invited to join as a neighbour at home of some of the crew. Then some of us joined many New Zealanders as we crowded into the Cathedral for the midnight service.

On Christmas Day itself, Whitbreads as sponsors had organised a party in which the whole fleet could join as a big family, bringing any friends they wished. A ferry had been chartered which took us all off to a delightful island bay, from whose private wharf we could walk up the hill, climb trees, bathe and enjoy a splendid Christmas picnic lunch. Then the band struck up in the saloon for dancing as the vessel cruised from one anchorage to the next; in some of them friends in their own yachts came alongside to join the party for a time. The Christmas cake was cut by Cornelius van Rietschoten, skipper of the leading yacht overall at that halfway mark, and our hosts were thanked by Clare Francis, who surely demonstrated the entente cordiale, as her French husband Jacques stood beside her. 'What a lovely, lovely Christmas', murmured one of her crew's mother, who had flown out from Scotland to join the fun in Auckland.

8 Storms to Cape Horn

The Prime Minister of New Zealand, the Rt. Hon. R. D. Muldoon, fired the gun from a Royal New Zealand Navy battery on the top of North Hill to signal the start of the third leg. 'From the starting line to Rio de Janiero leaving "A" buoy to starboard and Cape Horn to port', read the sailing instructions. The starting line was between North Hill and Bean Rock Lighthouse in the entrance to Auckland. 'A' buoy is three miles along the approach channel, Cape Horn 5,500 miles from there, while Rio is 7,400 miles from the start.

It was 11 a.m. on 26 December, an early summer day of sparkling blue sea and fine weather clouds, with a warm breeze. All Auckland was on holiday for the day following Christmas, and it seemed that those who

possibly could get there either packed every vantage point around the harbour, or went afloat on the harbour itself.

The police forecast proved correct that an enormous number of local craft of all sizes would turn out to watch the start. Equally the Royal New Zealand Yacht Squadron opinion that many cruising yachtsmen would have gone off cruising over the Christmas holiday proved correct; yet all through the morning groups of them had been sailing back from neighbouring islands and anchorages to converge on the start area, or to intercept the racers on their first few miles of the race.

Debenhams had been the first to leave her moorings, cheered by her fellow competitors as she passed them, while hundreds of well

The start off Auckland was a great festival of boats.

wishers waved from Marsden Wharf. She sailed out to inspect the start line; 'Very crowded and difficult to see marks of the course', her log recorded, in the handwriting of Alan Green, her navigator in the place of Tom Woodfield, who had flown back to London for his duties with Trinity House; Alan Green had recently been selected for the important post as secretary of the Royal Ocean Racing Club, and was taking an ocean racing holiday in the Southern Ocean before assuming his duties on return.

The actual starting area was reasonably clear of spectator craft, but several skippers found it hard to make out the buoys placed as distance marks, and combined with the tidal stream behind them, it proved extra difficult to make a perfect start.

Indeed the Prime Minister's starting gun was followed by a second gun, and international pennant O was broken out from the flagstaff on the top of North Head. This meant that some yachts were over the start line too early, but it was left to each yacht to decide whether to turn back or not. Even those watching from near the flagstaff were uncertain, so close were several of the fleet to the line; but the judge, with his eye fixed to binoculars exactly along the starting line, ruled without hesitation that *G.B.II* was several feet over the line, while *33 Export* was just over. However, both sailed on, so the race committee awarded penalties of ten minutes to be added to the time of *G.B.II* and five minutes against *33 Export*.

Twenty minutes later there was a hum of tense excitement as it was seen that *Disque D'Or* was sailing back from the group of competitors rounding 'A' buoy. She had been on the right side of the line at the start, so many watchers were apprehensive lest someone onboard had been injured; others had different suggestions. 'Perhaps something vital has been

The start was signalled by the Prime Minister of New Zealand from the top of North Hill.

left behind—the chart of Cape Horn, or the skipper's antarctic clothing?'

Then as she sailed over the start line, she rounded up and set off in chase. It seemed that a radio broadcast of the start gave those onboard the false impression that it was she that was over the line at the gun, and after general discussion onboard it was decided to go back to make certain. Fortunately this did not in the end hit her too hard, as she caught up with the fleet when it was held up by calms next day.

That first day gave a good easterly breeze as the fleet sailed hard on the wind across Hauraki Gulf. This was no open ocean work, but the chops of shallow and tidal water caused nausea to some of those who had already sailed half way round the world without feeling seasick; a long spell in harbour finishing off with Christmas festivities leaves stomachs particularly vulnerable until sea legs are regained.

With Leslie Williams back as skipper of *Heath's Condor*, after his leg and leg about with Robin Knox-Johnston, she sailed with two reefs in the mainsail and cutter rig to catch *Pen Duick VI* off Caromandel, but fell astern of her again tacking to windward towards Great Mercury Island, when Eric Tabarly took a course among the islands close inshore.

Heath's Condor logged that first evening, 'A day highlighted by all the emotions of leaving Auckland after four very happy weeks. The start was spectacular because of the wind, the sunshine and the huge spectator fleet. The easterly wind made for some hard sailing from which we gained considerably against *G.B.II*, but *Pen Duick* pointed better and got ahead.'

Yet *Flyer*, following up the trio of maxi-yachts, reported differently: '*Pen Duick* appears to be a fast boat in light airs, but doesn't point very high.' As they passed 100 metres off Stanley Island in bright moonlight, *Flyer*

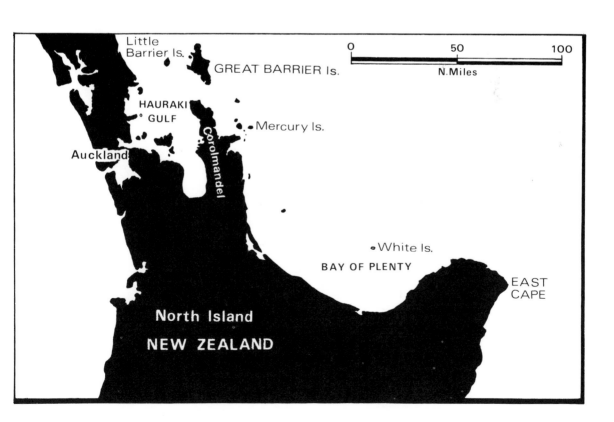

Cape Horn to Port

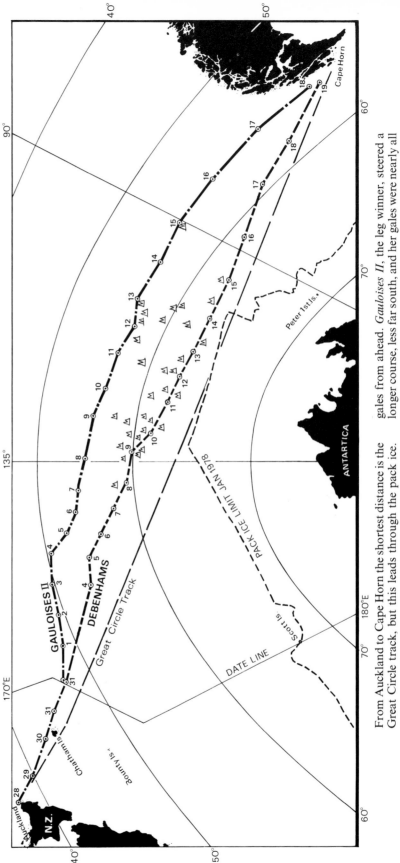

From Auckland to Cape Horn the shortest distance is the Great Circle track, but this leads through the pack ice. *Debenhams* steered near to this track, just missing the pack ice; she met numerous icebergs and some easterly gales from ahead. *Gauloises II*, the leg winner, steered a longer course, less far south, and her gales were nearly all from astern.

104

recorded of her old rival *Kings Legend* 'breathing down our neck, but we pulled away, hard on the wind in a short steep sea'.

With the dawn on 27 December the leaders ran into calm, and those astern came up to join them lying in the middle of the Bay of Plenty, near White Island, with its volcanic plume of white smoke. *Flyer* came up to 200 metres from *G.B.II* with *Heath's Condor* one mile ahead, *Kings Legend* and *Neptune* astern. 'Turned complete circle,' logged *ADC Accutrac*, 'so did *Gauloises*'. 'No sight of *Pen Duick*' logged *Heath's Condor*, yet the French yacht at the same time identified *Heath's Condor* away to leeward. Then the wind came again, still from ahead as they tacked towards East Cape. *Flyer* logged 'Wonderful sailing—full moon—clear sky—gentle wind—porpoises around the boat—New Zealand is giving us a real farewell.'

East Cape was the departure point from New Zealand. 'To Cape Horn 4,270 miles' logged *ADC Accutrac*. Thoughts turned to a message received just before leaving Auckland, cabled from Captain Oram, President of the International Association of Cape Horners; this sent to all skippers and crews of the yachts the association's warmest Christmas greetings and good wishes for a safe and successful rounding of Cape Horn. Such a salute from a group, all of whose members had themselves rounded Cape Horn under sail, was surely an encouragement.

'We seem to be able to outsail *G.B.II*' recorded *Flyer* next day, 'in anything from force 3 downwards,' *Pen Duick* and *Heath's Condor* were still in sight and *Kings Legend* was not far astern. Following these leaders much of the fleet was bunched, with many sightings and various changes of fortune in the light easterly conditions that prevailed with a high pressure area moving slowly along their track.

'Crossed 180th meridian—thinking backwards now', logged *ADC Accutrac* as her longitude changed from east to west and began to decrease on an east-going course. *Heath's Condor* and *Adventure* had changed their calendars at this point so that they had 28 December twice; however, in this latitude the official date line is diverted to the eastwards so that Chatham and various other islands can share their dates with New Zealand; most of the fleet conformed to this calendar, so for a day or two one might be sailing on Thursday, while for another yacht in sight of her it would still be Wednesday.

Chatham Island lay directly on the track and was sighted some 20 miles to the north by *G.B.II* on 30 December, that is four days after the start. The group lies right out in the Pacific Ocean, and some 650 miles by sea from Auckland; it consists of Chatham Island itself, or Whairikaun, 38 miles long and 25 across, with land rising up to 1,000 feet high; also the smaller Pitt Island or Rangihaute, and South-East Island or Rangatira, besides many rocks and shoals.

Most of the fleet gave a good clearance to the group, but *Kings Legend* ventured right among the rocks to gain advantage from a local tidal stream of two to three knots; she also had a radio conversation with a Chatham islander whose livelihood was sheep farming and fishing.

The light easterlies were still holding as the fleet approached the official date line on 170° east, so this meant an extra day for those still to change. Thus *Debenhams* logged 'New Year's Eve party—super ice cake, Bolinger champagne and lots of laughs'; yet next day was another New Year's Eve as its date was also 31 December. By then the barometer was falling fast and a rain squall followed a roll of grey-white clouds. That evening was quite a different type of New Year's Eve party as the sea became rougher with a rising wind. Before midnight she logged 'This squall is a good 'un—force 10', and her barometer reached its trough soon afterwards.

'A happy New Year', logged *ADC Accutrac* just after midnight by the new calendar; it was blowing a gale and soon afterwards her No 3

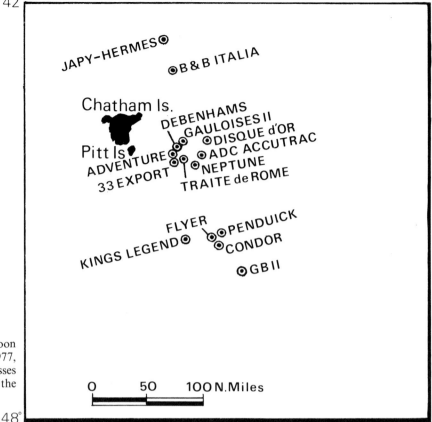

42°

JAPY-HERMES ◎

◎ B & B ITALIA

Chatham Is.

DEBENHAMS
GAULOISES II
◎ DISQUE d'OR
◎ ADC ACCUTRAC
Pitt Is.
ADVENTURE ◎◎ ◎ NEPTUNE
33 EXPORT
TRAITE de ROME

FLYER
◎◎ PENDUICK
KINGS LEGEND ◎ ◎◎ CONDOR

◎ GB II

48°

170°

Positions of the yachts at noon (G.M.T.)—30 December 1977, and (right) *Heath's Condor* passes some of the outlying rocks in the Chatham Island group.

0   50   100 N.Miles

jib top blew out. *Heath's Condor* had her New Year's Eve party, including Christmas pudding and the Major's brandy sauce, with three reefs in the main and storm rig before the mast. Earlier that day the wind had fallen to almost calm, so the skipper insisted on a sacrifice to King Neptune for better winds; Justin Smart, youngest member of the crew, was ordered to throw overboard his much prized oxygen-giving plant, and very soon afterwards it was blowing a gale. Yet King Neptune seemed not too pleased with the offering, or possibly the order had been disobeyed, as the storm persisted from right ahead and on New Year's day the mainsail had to be lowered to reduce speed as the yacht was pounding so heavily in heavy, confused seas. A great deal of water was coming below through the fore hatches and round the mast, so continuous pumping was necessary.

By this time *G.B.II* was well ahead of the fleet, under a storm jib with two reefs in the mainsail. Then her barometer began to rise, without change in wind direction. Under the violence of the storm her mainsail track, holding the sail close to the mast, broke two-thirds of the way up; she was left sailing to windward under storm jib alone, and as her log was out of action throughout that gale, she could only guess at the distance made good.

'Life is difficult onboard, but still well organized,' logged *Flyer*, sailing with three reefs in the mainsail, three in the mizzen and a small jib. As the wind showed signs of veering, one strand of a lower shroud broke, but she kept going just the same. She recorded that the depression responsible for the gale was only overtaking very slowly, and she correctly forecast that a long blow could be expected.

'What did you do yourself, personally, in

106

such a frightful storm?' someone asked the skipper of *Flyer* when she reached harbour about a month later.

'Crossword puzzles,' answered Cornelius van Rietschoten.

Kings Legend was also forced to slow down when the yacht began to plunge from the tops of waves into the troughs. 'Wind 50 knots, Ya-Hoo,' she recorded. Then, just like her rival *Flyer*, a strand broke in a lower shroud; she bore away for an hour to ease the strain, but in spite of all this achieved an excellent 423 miles during two days of the gale at its height. Yet *Flyer* logged 425 miles.

33 Export, with hopes of repeating her victory of the previous leg, was well up in the main group as they passed Chatham Isles, and her barometer had slumped to its low of 981 mb with the wind blowing a modest force 3 from ahead. Suddenly it increased to gale force

with little change of direction, then gradually strengthened until 30 hours later it was a full storm; it was at the height of this that she suffered a really bad knockdown.

Here is the story as told by Sylvi Delinondes, a girl in her crew; she wrote it in French, so this is a translation.

'On 1 January the wind increased from ahead during the evening, and reached around 45 knots. We were under number three yankee and mainsail with four reefs. The sea got up very fast. On 2 January the sea continued to mount and the wind force reached 65 knots. Towards six in the morning we were relaxed, the boat under very reduced sail was travelling well, and everything was under control. Jean Claude and Michel made themselves breakfast, Eric, Dave Lavie and Thomas were on watch, the others were sleeping.

Suddenly there was a tremendous bang, and

107

the boat was thrown on her side, in fact she may have even turned right over. Rapidly we recovered ourselves, but what a sight! The chart table had emptied itself into the W.C. The charts, pencils, notebooks and navigation books, barometer—everything!

The tool chest had been emptied and the spanners, files, rasps and screwdrivers had stuck themselves into the ceiling of the galley. The floorboards had all come adrift and tins of food had been scattered everywhere. Water, which had been forced in by the knock-down, was up to the floorboards. In the saloon, the batteries had broken their straps and their boxes had smashed the floor of the saloon; one had then catapulted into the lee bunk, the pieces landing on Philippe Schaff who was sleeping. He was injured in the stomach.

Every container had emptied itself. It was an appalling mess!

We learnt later, after it was all over, that all had been going well and that the boat had been handling easily.

But without warning a wave approached like a wall, absolutely vertical, many metres high. It had not broken, but, it seems hardly possible, the wave rolled over the decks, taking the whole boat with it.

From the trajectory of the displaced clothing, batteries and tools, we worked out that the boat must have rolled 140°.'

What a story she told, and what an amazing crew to press on with scarcely a pause. As they set about pumping out the water and getting some order below, the storm continued to increase in violence; yet it veered to south so she was able to sail an easterly course at fine speed, covering 197 miles in the day—knockdown and all.

Adventure had only one 31 December, having changed her date three days earlier. Thus on her New Year's Eve the wind increased to force 7, but the boat was going fairly well to windward. 'No problems,' she logged.

Yet in the early hours of the next day, with the gale steadily increasing from force 9 to force 10, she logged 'Boat slamming badly—fore hatch strongback broke.' As the storm veered in direction to south, it became very cold and goggles were required by the helmsman; it was cold enough down below with the boat taking water through the damaged fore hatch, but it was soon realised that a great deal more water was coming from a leak below the waterline. It is scarcely possible to find where the water comes from when it is being hurled around, as the yachts slam and lurch; it was not until four days later that the leak was confirmed as two cracks in the GRP hull where the trailing edge of the keel was faired into the bilge, and in the area of the boat where the original trim tab had been glassed in.

Ian Bailey Willmot, her skipper, wrote afterwards 'The rate of pumping needed to keep up with the water steadily increased throughout the remainder of leg 3. Although the condition never became critical it was very worrying not knowing how far the problem would deteriorate.'

Worrying indeed. There could be no turning back against the prevailing westerlies, and there was no accessible harbour within thousands of miles. Logically the best thing was to sail on, keeping up with the fleet, as this gave the best chance of help should the leak become very much worse. Yet it must have needed a skipper thoroughly confident of his crew and his own seamanship to drive on, taking a track through the icy waters of the Southern Ocean.

Skippers and crews were not the only people to have worries when the yachts were far from any harbour or even shipping route in the Southern Ocean. Parents, friends, employers, sponsors and many other well-wishers were anxious for news and looking forward to hearing that their particular yacht was safely round the Horn. To help them, either directly or through the Press, Race Control was established in the R.N.S.A.'s headquarters at Portsmouth, and anyone ringing it at any time of the day or night could get the latest information, so long as any of the yachts were

Race control kept track of all the yachts, and coped with a barrage of enquiries. Left to right George Ward, Mike Dewe, John Wharton and Gordon Townshend.

still at sea. Race Control was manned by a team of volunteers from the membership of the Association, each taking turns of duty. Radio reports direct from the yachts, or sometimes through their sponsors in London, Paris or elsewhere were recorded in Race Control on a large state board, while charts of the course showed the latest reported position of yachts, with different coloured tapes tracing out their course.

Often the Race Controller on duty was kept fully occupied recording and plotting the information as it came in, while the telephones were constantly ringing for information. To help out, telephone tapes were installed so that if the duty controller was already occupied a taped message of the latest position was broadcast to the caller without delay. When inquiries concerned matters of race policy, they were usually handed on to Captain Norman, the race secretary, who sometimes had calls which may have been put through at civilized hours in New York, New Zealand or elsewhere, yet pulled him from his bed in

England. Often enough a representative of the Race Committee was required to answer problems on radio or television in various countries. In these, and many other cases, Dudley Norman would discuss the problem with the Race Chairman, or whoever was acting as his deputy in England when Admiral Steiner was at the stop-overs.

B and B Italia recorded 50 knots of wind in that same New Year's day gale; *Pen Duick VI* logged 55 knots, which is the upper limit of force 10 on the Beaufort scale; on board *Gauloises II* it went up to 60 knots, which is within the range of violent storm. None escaped a severe and protracted blow, with exceptionally high seas.

The wind direction was not the same for all; for most of the fleet the wind veered to south or even south-by-west as it reached its height. For those which kept further south the wind remained ahead throughout the storm. Thus *Flyer* had 32 hours of gale force from the south-south-east, then another day of stiff breeze still close-hauled, and yet a further day of moderate to light wind from the same direction. *Heath's Condor* had similar conditions, but logged 27 miles less in three days. In the same three days *Kings Legend* logged four miles less than *Flyer*; she was further south still and also had headwinds throughout.

Gauloises II was sailing hard on the wind when the gale struck; she ran off slightly on an easterly course, and her wind veered to south. When it reached its height of 60 knots, it veered further to south-south-west to bring it abaft the beam; for her, then 150 miles northwards of *Kings Legend*, the gale continued for nearly another day, so that she logged gale force winds for 48 hours compared with 32 hours for *Flyer* and *Kings Legend*.

This must have given *Gauloises II* a particularly severe trial, but her crew brought her through it without damage, and it left her in a strong position in relation to her fellow competitors. By the time the storm died down she was probably in the lead, allowing for handicap, with *Flyer* competing hard, and next *Traite de Rome*, which had also been north of the low centre, but further from it as her barometer did not fall so low and her wind speed not quite so high.

As conditions moderated in the Southern Ocean, the scene must shift to London where the race committee sat to consider the problem of *Pen Duick* as the protest committee in New Zealand had ruled that she was provisionally eligible, subject to her rating certificate being found valid. This could not be decided in New Zealand as the rating certificate submitted by *Pen Duick* was not available there; in addition it was felt that advice should be sought from the Offshore Racing Council, the international body which controls ocean racing and its special rules. It was also considered essential that the full Race Committee should make the decision, as the New Zealand protest committee had made it clear that validity of the rating certificate was the deciding factor over eligibility.

There is no doubt that members of the Race Committee sincerely hoped that a way could be found within the rules to make *Pen Duick's* entry eligible. Yet the committee had declared that the race should be sailed under international rules, and it therefore had no right to change these. It found that the rating certificate offered by *Pen Duick VI* was not valid, as it expired on 30 November 1977, or 26 days before the race started for her; valid, it was decided, could only be interpreted as being valid at the start of that yacht in the race.

Thus it was announced that *Pen Duick* could still not be considered eligible; however, the opportunity was still open for her owner's representative in Paris to produce an unexpired valid certificate from the French rating authority.

There was so much general interest in *Pen Duick's* eligibility that the Race Committee published an announcement that her rating certificate could not be considered valid. The committee made no mention of disqualification, as an invalid certificate meant that her entry had not been accepted, and obviously a yacht cannot be disqualified from a race in which she is not entered. However, unofficial news reached the yachts in the Southern Ocean using the word 'disqualification', and this caused such uneasiness among some of them that an English yacht, *ADC Accutrac*, cabled reporting this and stressing the hope that *Pen Duick* be allowed to continue racing.

Another English yacht passed on to *Pen Duick* the incorrect news that she was disqualified. We have already seen that before leaving Auckland, Eric Tabarly had been told that the eligibility of his entry was uncertain, and if his rating certificate was found invalid he could not receive any of the official prizes; he was told that meantime he was welcome to join in the race and would receive all the support and facilities that went with it.

A day or two later a further rating certificate was received from Paris, bringing up to date the one which was expired. However, the situation remained that the yacht had in her keel uranium with higher specific gravity than lead. This had been allowed at the time *Pen Duick VI* was launched, and indeed when she had previously competed in races organised by the R.N.S.A.; yet the Offshore Racing Council advised that the rules had since been changed to preclude the issue of a rating certificate to a yacht with keel material heavier than lead. It informed the Race Committee that this applied, even for a yacht which had previously been allowed a certificate; it also advised that the National Offshore Rating Authority for *Pen Duick VI* had been informed that her certificate could not be considered valid.

Such evidence, coming from the international body responsible for making the offshore racing rules, was clear and authoritative. The Race Committee remain the judges to make the decision on whether the yacht is eligible to start or continue in a race, but there was no reasonable alternative but for it to follow the advice of the Offshore Racing Council and rule that *Pen Duick VI* was not eligible. Indeed this definite decision was announced before any yacht completed the course.

Back to the Southern Ocean, where the yachts were enjoying good weather after the storm. 'Gale over, no damage to us; stayed in racing trim all the time, as did *Flyer*, we suspect', logged *Kings Legend*. In fact we have already seen that *Flyer* had suffered a broken strand in one of her lower shrouds, but she lost no distance from this and the damaged shroud was soon replaced by a new wire. 'All systems are A1,' *Flyer* logged, 'quite warm and pleasant on deck; we hope other boats have the same calm.'

'Bird life returning,' logged *ADC Accutrac*, 'Mostly albatrosses and shearwaters.' Next day—it was 6 January—she recorded half way to the Horn. *Adventure* reported a large whale astern, and with the calmer weather was able to locate her hull leak in the vicinity of her old trim tab; but it still needed at least two hundred pumps each hour and sometimes as much as 1,000; with so much work for them, three of her five pumps became unserviceable. *Debenhams* also commented on a large whale close to her, but fortunately it was unperturbed; her crew seemed more perturbed by their lack of wind, giving her a run of only 141 miles on a day when *ADC Accutrac* covered 50 miles more.

The first ice, seen by *G.B.II*, was in the early hours of 7 January and that day she saw eight more bergs around 59° south latitude; she was leading the fleet and about 100 miles closer to Cape Horn than *Heath's Condor*, which met her first ice the following day; 'spectacular close view of a large iceberg plus its accompanying growlers,' she logged.

In early January, around 60° south, there was some light even at midnight, so icebergs added variety to the view, and presented far less hazard than on the leg from Cape Town to New Zealand, when earlier in the year there were several hours of darkness.

Positions on 7 January 1978, a critical day for the race result.

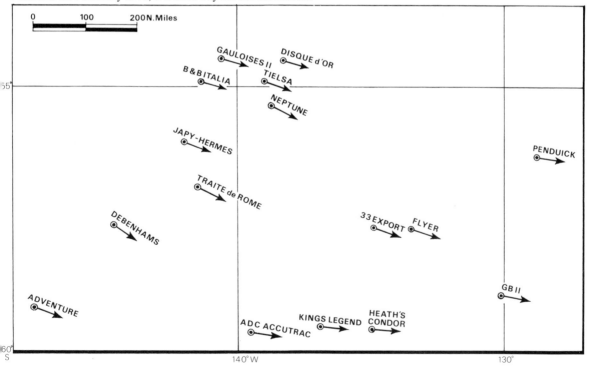

Debenhams once more saw most of the ice. She is here seen sailing past a berg, taken by Tony Dallimore from an inflatable dinghy rowed by Marie Christine Ridgway.

A critical day for the race result was 7 January. *G.B.II*, leading the fleet among the icebergs, had light winds from a northerly direction. About level with her, but 160 miles to the north, *Pen Duick VI* was sailing very fast before a westerly gale which gave up to 50 knots of wind; in the next three days she covered 791 miles while *G.B.II* covered only 623. Also in the northern group, following the general track of *Pen Duick*, came *Neptune* which recorded westerly gales on 7 January, and in the three succeeding days covered 703 miles of fast sailing. On the most northerly track of all at this stage was *Disque D'Or*, which enjoyed excellent fast sailing, while almost in her wake came *Gauloises II*, which sailed 719 miles in the next three days to put her into a strongly competitive position, considering that her handicap rating was ten feet less than *Flyer* and 30 feet less than *G.B.II*.

Once more it was *Debenhams* that saw most of the ice, as her modified great circle course took her down to 63° south. Her first berg was right ahead on 10 January when the inflatable dinghy was launched with Marie Christine onboard to photograph the yacht among the ice. The wind was quiet, but the sea was far from calm; not many women can have paddled their rubber dinghies among icebergs of the Southern Ocean on the way to sail round Cape Horn. This was a full day of interest for *Debenhams*; apart from several icebergs, she had heavy snow and a stiff wind an hour or two after the dinghy venture; at other times she sighted silver-grey petrels and sooty albatrosses; finally there was a tremendous birthday party for Noel Smart, with the hope that they might be off Cape Horn itself for Marie Christine's birthday party in seven days time.

For *ADC Accutrac*, about 140 miles ahead and in the same latitude, 10 January was not such a good day. The wind was light and mostly ahead, while the snow and frozen spray made it necessary for the helmsman to wear goggles to be able to see what was going on. She covered only 130 miles to noon, which turned out to be her shortest daily run on the leg, as well as her furthest south. Her consolation was that the barometer, already low at 984 mb, was dropping with the promise of a blow to come.

Kings Legend running fast before a Southern Ocean gale.

This promise was realised, but at first it came as a smack in the face, with a south-easter blowing from the pack ice and putting her hard on the wind. She lowered the mainsail and set a storm staysail, as the wind veered to south and piped up to a strong gale when she was passing a mile-long iceberg. The barometer checked its fall at 975 mb, so she hoisted a trisail and lowered the reefed mizzen; then as the barometer began to rise the gale reached storm force, another mile-long iceberg came in sight fairly close on her lee side, 'phenomenally impressive seas breaking over the top—approx 80 ft high,' she logged. Six hours later the wind had reached force 11—violent storm—blowing from due west; it was not quite so cold from that direction but there was no longer any lee from the pack ice, so very large seas built up. Through another night the gale gradually moderated, with the crew working hard to increase her sail step by step.

That same gale caught *G.B.II* on 11 January; she was in about the same latitude as *ADC Accutrac* but some 350 miles to the east; much of the time it blew from east-north-east to make

it really hard sailing. *Heath's Condor*, some 120 miles back from *G.B.II*, also had an easterly gale at the same time, while *Flyer*, on a track slightly to the northwards of *G.B.II*, but 85 miles astern of her, also had a strong gale, gusting to 60 knots; for her it came mostly from a westerly sector to help her on the way. *Flyer*'s log reported 'fabulous surfing at last,' but in the following watch a vicious squall tore her new flanker sail to pieces. Then two hours later 'Wind is gusting to 55 knots now and still increasing'; later, with the wind gusting to 60 knots she was surfing at high speeds on mountainous waves with two reefs in the mainsail and her jib top set. She also sighted an iceberg in the storm with waves breaking over it; 'This is how we expected the Southern Ocean to look.'

Certainly *ADC Accutrac* had the worst of that gale, but *Debenhams*, 120 miles to the south of her, had none of it, nor easterly wind either; indeed her winds during that period were no more than moderate. Yet 120 miles is really quite a distance apart; for instance a gale in the Scilly Isles and moderate winds off

Ushant would not be unusual, any more than a gale in Long Island Sound with moderate winds in Delaware Bay.

Yachts well to the north of *ADC Accutrac* also got no gale from 10 to 12 January, although they enjoyed strong following winds which persisted well. However, those well south had missed out on *Pen Duick's* storm of the previous week, which hit the northern group to drive them ahead.

The positions shown on the chart for 12 January 1978 are approximate as several yachts had not been able to take any sights for two or three days. Yet it is clear that *Heath's Condor*, to the south, had lost a great deal compared with *Pen Duick*, well to the north of her, and she was scarcely nearer to Cape Horn than the group led by *Neptune*, with *Gauloises II* and *33 Export* both strongly placed allowing for their handicaps. *Flyer* had made up on *G.B.II*, and even more important to her, had gained a substantial margin over her special rival *Kings Legend*, whose crew were the only ones to know this as her main radio transmitter had been out of action since 7 January.

There was still a final Southern Ocean storm to come, making the fourth since leaving New Zealand. It first struck *Debenhams*, sailing through ice and snow in 62° south; the wind reached force 8 and above, with streaks of foam forming on the sea in a line with the wind, over a cross swell. She passed an iceberg at the height of the gale, with the sea temperature only half a degree above freezing point; but fortunately there was little spray over the deck as she ran at an exciting speed to give her fastest three-day run of the leg.

Next to the south on 15 January was *Adventure*, which had just passed through a field of growlers with the midnight dusk making them hard to see. The wind shrieked at her, reaching nearly storm force, with gusts up to 55 knots; yet the boat coped well, although the rough seas put the pumping rate up to 1,000 strokes on the whale pumps each hour.

For those ahead and further north the gale caught them the following day. Thus *ADC Accutrac* recorded on 16 January about the same conditions as *Adventure's* of the previous day. The further north they were the more moderate the gale; *B & B Italia* in 55°33' recorded the wind as 35 knots, while *Gauloises II* in much the same latitude, recorded on 16 January her wind as 40 knots; she held

Position on 12 January shows those to the south loosing ground.

moderate gale for three days to give her a superbly good run to the Horn.

The leaders were too far ahead to benefit from this gale. On 15 January *Pen Duick VI* was headed by a 25 knot north-easter as she came up to Diego Ramirez; yet at 6 p.m. local time that evening she passed 10 miles south of Cape Horn, 21 days out of Auckland. This was an outstanding achievement partly due to fine sailing and partly her winning strategy, as although her northerly course was 200 miles longer than those keeping as close as they could to the great circle, she had practically no headwinds after the storm of 2 January.

Next day, 16 January, *G.B.II* rounded the Horn three miles off with squalls blowing up to force 7, while a force 10 squall hit her three hours afterwards. Her passage from Auckland to the Horn had been exciting enough; we have seen how the storm of 1 January had broken her main mast track, she had sighted many icebergs, then as the gale of 12 January moderated her steering cable broke, but was quickly replaced.

As *G.B.II* came up to the Horn, *Flyer* was 137 miles astern of her and competing hotly with *Heath's Condor*, coming up from further south. Indeed they mutually arranged extra radio routines as it seemed that they might actually meet at the Horn. *Flyer's* log, as always, makes excellent reading, but particularly so on that thrilling race to the Horn. 'Hail and snow showers—the deck is dangerous to work on, though the snow balls give some fun'. The wind was up to 30 knots, then in a windshift dropped down to a miserable 10. More snow, and the wind died completely.

More snow, and this time the wind died with it.

Allan Prior with a snow penguin on *Heath's Condor*'s deck.

Diego Ramirez Islands lie some 50 miles southwards of Cape Horn.

Next 'the sun comes through and it is a beautiful morning'; this allowed a good fix, but the shifting wind made it difficult to find a good heading for the Horn. Then the wind settled at north-west—force 7—and full speed for the Horn, 'everybody is in a good mood'. Later her log recorded a distinct change in the colour of the water—from the green-grey tint of the Southern Ocean to a more brown tint.

Meantime, *Heath's Condor* calculated that she would catch *Flyer* before the Horn if the wind held. Her log was also a joy to read, as she too, recorded fierce squalls, shifting winds and snow; her crew also had a snowball fight, but went further in building a snow penguin on deck; this was interrupted by sharp avoiding action as the helmsman turned to miss two large whales. Also, like *Flyer*, the sky cleared for a good star fix from which to plot an accurate course to the Horn, if the wind would only let her hold it.

Just as with *Pen Duick* the day before, the wind headed *Flyer* in the Horn area. Sailing against a light easterly, with a high swell still

from the west to shake much of the wind from the sails, she beat close-hauled through the channel, only a mile wide, between two groups of Diego Ramirez Isles; to her starboard was the 620 foot high Bartolomé, and to port North Rock. 'Beautiful, but grim sight, these rocks in the ocean', she logged.

Just as *Flyer* cleared Diego Ramirez, the island group was sighted by *Heath's Condor*; she passed a mile to the south and soon afterwards logged 'coast of Tierra del Fuego, snow covered mountains and Cabo de Hornos in sight'. The visibility must have been excellent as the group is 50 miles from Cape Horn.

For both of them the wind went back to south-west before they reached the Horn; *Flyer* passed 2 miles south of it at 4 p.m. local time 'moving with full speed. The Horn is a sight nobody will easily forget'. Only 12 miles astern of her was *Heath's Condor* and she logged 'very fast and exhilarating passage past the Horn—wind continually freshening and squally.' That evening she caught sight of a light ahead. It was *Flyer*, whose watch on deck had been caught

116

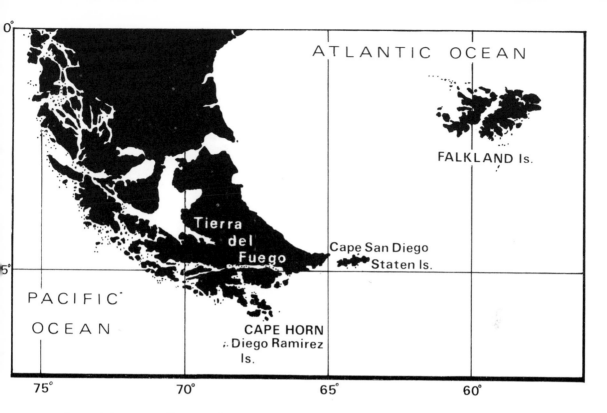

unaware by a vicious squall—'our first chinese gybe this race' she logged.

Wednesday 18 January was surely the day of the Horn, when half the fleet sailed past it within a period of 12 hours. In mid-morning *Disque D'Or* logged Cape Horn to port; this put her, on handicap, next to *Flyer* which led her round. Then came *Neptune*, on handicap only half an hour behind *Flyer*; she was followed shortly by *Tielsa*, and at 6.20 p.m. local time, *ADC Accutrac* left Cape Horn 1½ miles to port, 'Exchanged our courtesies to it with a six gun champagne cork salute'; her log also recorded that her cabin heater was not working, but 'morale still high due to high standard of food and Bumble's wonderful cooking'.

Two hours later came *Gauloises II* and she jumped to the head of the handicap order, a day ahead on corrected time of any yacht already round. Her rounding was exciting enough for anyone, as just short of the Horn itself, when Eric Loiseau was at the chart table, she almost pitch poled, which means that a big breaking sea throws up the stern to somersault over the bows. Fortunately it did not quite come to this disaster, but she started to drive herself under, then turned over in a broach with the foredeck and several feet of the mast under water. 'Chaviré—mât et tangon sous l'eau' made a dramatic log entry of the capsize beside 'Cape Horn par le travers babord à 2'. She was flying a spinnaker at the time, so much of this and its spinnaker pole went under water, putting a fantastic strain on the mast, which was twisted; but no other damage was done. This surely showed the great strength of this yacht and her fittings, besides the thoroughly seamanlike way in which she had been prepared for the severe trials of the race.

Everyone wanted a close up view of the Horn, yet usually the seas would be steeper in the relatively shallow water off it than in the open ocean. Long periods of strong westerly winds in the open ocean will often generate waves as long as 300 metres, and at this length they will begin to be affected by the bottom when the depth comes down to about 80

117

Cape Horn to port: David Alan-Williams rounds the Horn onboard *Heath's Condor* in excellent visibility, but soon afterwards the land was blotted out by vicious squalls.

fathoms; the effect then is that the wave period remains the same, but the length decreases and thereby makes the waves steeper. This alone is likely to make the seas more dangerous when the ocean bed comes up fairly rapidly from some thousand fathoms to a shelf of well under 100 fathoms, between Diego Ramirez and Cape Horn. In addition to this there is the Cape Horn current running between Diego Ramirez and the Horn, and seas always become more agitated when gales blow over a current.

Gauloises II was on this shelf when she so nearly pitch poled. Astern of *Gauloises II* came *Kings Legend* leaving Cape Horn a comfortable distance to port, which was tactically sound and the darkness in any case deprived her crew of a close up view; at least one of them had seen it already, as Bill Porter was making his third rounding of the Horn under sail, which must make him the doyen among ocean race crews.

Following astern of *Kings Legend* and in sight of her came *33 Export*; they rounded the Horn close enough to each other, but by first light next morning they were to be very much closer still. *33 Export* surfed into second place on handicap, but *Traite de Rome* was to better her by five hours on handicap when she rounded the Horn 17 hours later, with *B & B Italia* actually rounding a couple of hours before her and *Japy-Hermes* a couple of hours later. By this time *Debenhams* was well past Diego Ramirez, while *Adventure* was, surprisingly, suffering from lack of wind which kept her from the Horn for another day.

Surely it would need to go back many decades to find a day when eight vessels rounded the Horn under sail, besides eight more a day or so before or later. Could the Cape Horners of old have believed that within a week the magic words 'Cape Horn abeam' could be logged by 16 sailing yachts, while 183 men and women would earn the right to be called Cape Horners—nearly all were amateur sailors and some had been complete novices only six months before.

9 South Atlantic Trials

With the Horn abeam, crews tended to relax; aboard *Heath's Condor* they put on funny hats; in *ADC Accutrac* they fired a salute in champagne corks; and in every yacht there was a feeling of relief. Perhaps for many the challenge of sailing around the Horn was one of the main reasons for coming at all, and this had been achieved.

Yet many of them soon enough had evidence that they had not left bad weather behind in the Southern Ocean. The sea temperature quickly got warmer, but they had another thousand miles to sail before clearing the extreme limit for icebergs in January and March.

Pen Duick, over a day ahead of any other at the Horn, was favoured with modest weather at least until she was clear of Tierra Del Fuego and had sailed round to the east of Staten Island. She then steered to pass eastwards of the Falkland Islands, as it turned out the only yacht to take this track, but before she was up with the Falklands the wind freshened to strong, with squalls up to 50 knots. It was this same disturbance which, we read in the last chapter, hit *G.B.II* just three hours after she passed Cape Horn itself on 16 January. In the early hours of the morning her storm spinnaker had to come down quickly as the wind shot up to force 10; yet by late breakfast time it was down to light airs from nearly ahead, as she made for Le Maire Strait, which separates Staten Island from Tierra del Fuego.

The tidal stream runs at up to three knots in the middle of Le Maire Strait, and much faster closer to land; when favourable it could be a big help, although when running to the south it would normally be better to steer to the east, well wide of Staten Island. However, even if the tide is favourable, the Strait is no easy short cut, a dangerous and heavy tide-race extends up to five miles out from Cape San Diego and there may also be heavy tide-rips on the Staten Island side of the Strait. If a gale blows up suddenly against the stream, the whole width of the Strait, some 16 miles across, can become dangerous for small craft.

However *G.B.II* led the way through safely in quiet conditions and, as she set her course westwards of the Falklands, it blew up to a tea-time half gale again.

Flyer, with *Heath's Condor* close astern of her, passed the Horn some 18 hours after *G.B.II*; they also were hit by vicious squalls soon afterwards. We heard in the last chapter how one of these caught *Flyer*'s sails on the wrong side in a 'Chinese gybe', a term derived from the Chinese junk which sometimes runs with parts of its battened sail on each gybe; this blew out *Flyer*'s spinnaker and damaged the slider of its pole. A flanker sail was set instead, but along came a 40 knot squall to blow that out too. 'This forces us down to a poled-out blast reacher—just as well for in Le Maire Strait a steep sea was running'. She passed Cape San Diego after a wild run through the Strait in the darkness.

At first daylight *Flyer*'s watch on deck saw

Staten Island to starboard as *Heath's Condor* made for Le Maire Strait.

the last of the snow peaked mountains disappear to the south, and there also was *Heath's Condor* only five miles astern. For a time she had lowered her running sail to carry only a reefed mainsail and so avoided any damage from the squalls, but Graham Pearson had to go aloft to clear the halyards, and she was still catching up *Flyer*. 'Magnificent sight of the snow covered peaks of Staten Island', she logged in the early morning.

Later that day both yachts sighted H.M.S. *Endurance*, which was operating in that area and sent her two helicopters over with film cameramen. *Heath's Condor* spoke on the radio to Colin Forbes, the film director who had followed the race round the world; several yachts had seen him peering out of aircraft at quite unexpected places, while he also had film cameras aboard several of the yachts.

It was 5 p.m., local time, 18 January before *Heath's Condor* at last caught up *Flyer*; her navigator, Gerard Dijkstra, appreciated that her rivals for handicap places were the lower rating yachts not far astern; he hoped for some tough windward work to give *Flyer* the chance to gain distance on them. Yet it was another day and night of overtime work by her 'sail loft' down below before the damage between Cape Horn and Le Maire Strait had been repaired.

Meantime other yachts were having a tough

time after passing Cape Horn. *ADC Accutrac* had scarcely completed her champagne cork salute to Cape Horn as she passed it one and half miles to port when, in a 40 knot squall she broached heavily first rolling 75° to windward, then hurtling through a 150° roll to lie 75° to leeward. It was all hands on deck to clear things before she ran on for Le Maire Strait under a poled-out jib before a full gale. Once settled again those off watch went below; over a cup of tea there were nervous giggles more than talk, as minds began to appreciate fully the dangers they had faced.

In the early morning she passed half a mile off Cape San Diego to get the best help from the stream; 'Still plenty of excitement after the Horn', she logged and well she might, as the Admiralty *Sailing Directions* advise that no small craft should go within five miles of the Cape as this race can be very dangerous, at times running up to 10 knots. However, when well clear of the Strait the wind fell to almost nothing as she came up with H.M.S. *Endurance* and her helicopters.

We have already heard how *Gauloises II* nearly pitch poled as she ran up towards Cape Horn; then she sailed on at great speed through Le Maire Strait, after which the wind fell to light when H.M.S. *Endurance* visited her.

Following along three hours after *Gauloises*

II, Kings Legend was sailing very fast before a full westerly gale with a boomed-out headsail and full mainsail; often she was picked up by a wave to surge ahead at 15 knots or more. In the darkness she sighted a light astern which was coming up so fast that her watch on deck thought it must be H.M.S. *Endurance*; yet first light disclosed that it was *33 Export*, flying a spinnaker and surging ahead with some incredible surfing.

Bill Porter was steering *Kings Legend* as *33 Export* came up abeam to leeward, seeming to be picked up on the face of almost every wave. A big wave came and *33 Export* swept ahead, then almost slowly she broached, to turn across the wave and lie practically stopped right across the bows of *Kings Legend*. Bill Porter looked down on her powerless; he knew that if the next wave should pick up *Kings Legend*, as about every third one had been doing, he could not possibly steer clear and his yacht would come down right on top of her. Not only would *33 Export* be smashed to pieces but her tough aluminium hull would certainly knock the bottom out of glass-fibre *Kings Legend*.

Those on deck in *33 Export* appeared to be absorbed in their own problems of the broach and were perhaps fortunately unaware of the Damacles sword balanced above them. Bill Porter had reacted immediately to put the wheel hard over; then time stood still with the horror of his situation. Would the next wave pick her up to surf down onto the boat below?

Perhaps the rudder hard over acted as something of a brake, or perhaps it was good fortune. Anyhow *Kings Legend* did not surf that time and, she was able to turn clear of *33 Export*'s stern.

After that *Kings Legend* set a spinnaker herself to get well away from her hard driving rival. It was still blowing a full gale but they were coming off the Cape Horn shelf into ocean depths again; so the seas were lengthening once more. 'Set chute as a sporting gesture, and finally left them behind', logged Skip Novak, her navigator.

For this pair, the stream in Le Maire Strait had turned against, so they steered south of Staten Island, with the gale actually increasing until they turned north off Cape St. Jean, where the South Atlantic Ocean greeted them with wind no more than a mere moderate breeze.

This course around Staten Island added some 30 miles to the distance, yet as they approached the Falklands next day *33 Export* came up with *ADC Accutrac*, which had passed the Horn six hours ahead and had also benefited from a favourable stream in Le Maire Strait. 'Crossed tacks with *33 Export*—she's going fantastically', logged John Tanner in *ADC Accutrac*. *Kings Legend* was also up with them, although she passed further westwards of the Falklands; certainly on this occasion the course outside Staten Island paid off handsomely. This is also shown by their daily run to noon as *ADC Accutrac* logged a modest 155 miles, after a miserable light breeze when the Royal Navy was chatting up the girls onboard; over the same period *Kings Legend* logged 222 miles. *33 Export* did even better as she played the currents among the Falkland Islands, passing through islets of the Jason Group.

ADC Accutrac also went among the Falkland Islands, passing two miles inside Grand Jason Island. Soon afterwards she blew out her storm spinnaker with yet another spectacular broach; it was just too soon for the cameras onboard the Antarctic cruise liner *World Discoverer*, which later closed to exchange courtesies.

The three yachts which rounded the Horn on 19 January, *B & B Italia*, *Traite de Rome* and *Japy-Hermes* had more moderate conditions until past Staten Island, although the wind whistled up to force 6 as *Traite de Rome* and *Japy-Hermes* went through Le Maire Strait.

It was just after midnight, on 20 January, local time that *Debenhams* passed the Horn, sighting its dim lighthouse only a mile or two away; for her the wind was squally, but no more than a moderate breeze as she sailed on, just to catch the tide in Le Maire Strait, before H.M.S. *Endurance* welcomed her to the Atlantic.

The following night, 21 January, conditions were almost too quiet for *Adventure* as she sighted H.M.S. *Endurance* just an hour after she had passed the Horn two miles to port. This certainly made the pumping easier, at least until clear of the Falkland Islands; but those of her bilge pumps still in action had a great deal more work to do later on.

Meantime there had been ample drama on ahead.

Back to 19 January, when the yachts passing the Horn were having moderate conditions, yet some 300 miles to the north *G.B.II* was being severely tested, It was bad enough when a storm force squall suddenly blew up from a mere half gale in the early hours of the morning. Then lightning struck her; Enrique Zulveta was hurled from the wheel to the deck, while Steve White, who was furling the mizzen sail, was thrown onto his back. Both watched,

with something more than apprehension, as they saw the masts glowing brightly, and they were quite surprised to find themselves uninjured. No one dared touch the steering wheel for a time, in case it was still 'live'.

When the helmsman took on again, steering seemed difficult until it was realised that the compass was all over the place. Robert James checked by astro bearings to find that the deviation was 70° east, so that when the helmsman steered the charted course for Rio he was actually pointing at Cape Town.

The wind indicator, was no longer any help to hold the course, as it and all the other electrical instruments on the mast had been burnt out and were useless. Even the electric log, so valuable to show the speed and distance run through the water, was out of action. 'I anticipate a slow erratic course with no instruments or compass', recorded Robert James in *G.B.II*'s log. At least the radio was undamaged and news of the accident was received by *Flyer* later that day.

H.M.S. Endurance and her helicopters made contact with most of the yachts in the Cape Horn area.

Yet the fears of *G.B.II*'s skipper were unfounded, as his crew soon showed that the skill gained from steering three-quarters of the way round the world with the help of the best instruments available, enabled them to make a good job of it with practically none at all. The compass deviation was changing so that, 12 hours after the lightning strike it had fallen from 70° to 55°, where it steadied so long as the course remained the same. All this made ample work for the navigator, but it also encouraged an alertness by all to notice the wind on the back of their necks, to keep an eye on the sun and stars, and gradually to develop a sixth sense for pointing in the right direction.

Far from a slow erratic course, her next three days gave the best runs of the race with 846 miles in the right direction. On the last of these, 21 January, she actually broke the 300 mark, with a day's run confirmed by sights as 304 miles; part of that terrific run had been in force 9—strong gale. Steering before this with no instruments was truly a feat of which even the most experienced helmsman could be proud.

It was also a great day for *Heath's Condor*, 150 miles astern. She covered an amazing 309 miles in the day to noon, but not without a great deal of hard work. During the middle watch, running under the gale spinnaker with one reef in the mainsail, she suffered a heavy broach in a squall. The boom preventer broke under pressure from a wave in the lee side of the mainsail and the cockpit was filled with water. All hands were called on deck as an emergency, the spinnaker was handed and a poled-out running sail was set with a large staysail. The wind and sea steadily increased in the next watch, in which she covered 52 miles. 'The wind has now reached gale force from behind—under this rig we run with good directional stability and very fast.'

It was still the Roaring Forties, and although nothing like so cold as in the Southern Ocean, the hours of darkness were much longer.

These were fantastic runs even with the help of the Falkland current. '2,044 miles in eight days' logged *G.B.II*. 'Grand day's sailing' recorded *Heath's Condor*. Yet the fact is that even these speeds were not enough to catch up the fastest of the low handicap yachts, should they be running under similar conditions. 300 miles a day for the big yachts would be matched by some 230 miles a day by *Gauloises II*, and she had already done well above that on one of her fast runs up to Cape Horn. To gain time on handicap over their low rating rivals, the maxi-yachts wanted hard beating to windward. They could expect little tough windward work before Rio, as once clear of the Roaring Forties, there would probably be the variables of the Horse Latitudes, with frequent calms.

However, *Flyer* was more than holding her own on handicap, in relation to the low rating boats, and was only slowly dropping astern on *Heath's Condor* in actual position. 'Fabulous sailing', she logged, but her crew was working very hard for it, with constant sail shifts to try and force the last foot of distance out of her; 'Set big boy instead of shooter, which remains a doubtful sail for a ketch—sometimes it works—sometimes it doesn't'. So often the sea and swell, just as much as the wind force and direction controlled which sail could be set.

Cornelius van Rietschoten, skipper of *Flyer*, would have liked to gain more easting to help the approach to Rio, then about a thousand miles ahead; but that would have meant running dead before the wind and she went faster with it on the quarter. Anyhow, she covered 775 miles in those three days, compared with 851 for *Heath's Condor*, a yacht some 12 feet longer.

Next day, it was 22 January, *G.B.II* ran out of the Roaring Forties. With only a light breeze in the morning, by the afternoon it was calm. She was in the Horse Latitudes; yet the following day showed that these can have gales as well as calms. By 6 a.m. the mainsail had to come down and soon she was beating against a northerly gale under her storm jib only, although the barometer was high and steady.

'A very bad sea almost necessitated heaving-to', logged Robert James. Another problem was that when she tacked to a course somewhere near east, there was no clue to what the deviation might be on that heading, although when the sun showed to allow an accurate check, the deviation was found to be nil on east, ranging to 45° east on north-west, which had been her course before tacking. Her gale persisted for 24 hours.

Pen Duick, on ahead, had a light easterly at this time but *Heath's Condor* also had a strong gale, which after a few hours dropped to nil; 'continued going nowhere for two hours with only the main up until the wind filled in from the north-west', she logged. By noon on 24 January, *G.B.II*, with just under 580 miles to Rio, was 224 miles closer to it than *Heath's Condor*; so, even with a dubious compass and no other instruments, her crew had every reason to feel that they could beat *Heath's Condor* this time.

ADC Accutrac was still in the Roaring Forties on 24 January and since her spectacular broach just after the Falklands, she had moderate weather compared with the really fast running conditions that the leading yachts had enjoyed. By the evening of 23 January she logged 'Lots of sail changes — mostly becalmed. Very confused seas — something coming'.

Come it did, when at 3 a.m. next morning, 24 January, it suddenly went from flat calm to 45 knots in the eye of a low. The main topping-lift parted and the mizzen sail blew out before they settled down with three reefs in the mainsail and a poled-out jib, running fast before a half gale from the south-south-west. A few hours later than mainsail ripped right across as she gybed; the crew had a tough time getting down the torn sail and setting the spare one. 'Who says the Southern Ocean's the worst', read the log after the gale had blown itself out, to leave a night of light airs and a morning of quiet breeze. Yet that evening another gale hit them. A huge storm cloud was seen approaching,

'just time to change down before it would have knocked us flat', *ADC Accutrac* logged.

Some 400 miles astern, *Adventure* was not so fortunate on just that same night. For her, it had been blowing gale force or over all that day, first from the north and then gradually backing to north-west. At 4 p.m. the storm was logged as force 10 to 11; force 11 is the Beaufort figure for violent storm with an average wind speed of about 60 knots. Now a 60 knot storm is something quite different from standing up clear of the windscreen in an open car travelling at 60 miles an hour on a calm day. A storm wind is a turbulent fury. A comparative lull may ease back to 40 knots or less; then a sudden gust hurtles at the boat at 20 knots or more above the average speed; no two gusts come from precisely the same direction. Added to this, 60 knots is equivalent to 68 land miles an hour, as a sea mile is a good deal longer than the land mile.

In the next four hours the storm became even fiercer and at 8 p.m. Ian Bailey-Willmot logged the wind as 11 to 12, which is near hurricane force. Ian is a professional naval officer with very many years at sea, including experience in command of his own warship; he is also renowned for his skill at driving very small ocean racers of the J.O.G. classes in thoroughly bad weather, so his assessment of conditions has exceptional authority. Here is his own account of what happened next.

'At 2230 on Wednesday 25 January the boat was broad-reaching under close reefed main (3 slabs) and storm jib. The wind was blowing 60 knots plus, but was beginning to moderate from earlier, when it was probably blowing 80 knots (the anemometer only reads up to 60). The sea conditions were particularly severe; although we had seen higher seas, I have never encountered seas as high and steep; I estimated the wave height at 45 feet. The sea was approaching the boat from the port quarter on a very dark night which precluded any avoiding manoeuvre by the helmsman; however the boat was coping with the conditions.'

John Kay was on deck in *Adventure* when she was knocked down, and lay over at 110° until the mainsail split.

'Suddenly she was knocked down. The boat rolled to 110° and stayed there. She only came up when the mainsail split along the full length of the foot.'

'John Kay and Phil Waters on deck were hurled against their safety harness, while Ian Mishelly was thrown off the wheel to finish up half over the side near the stern pulpit, at the full extent of his life line.'

'Down below the boat was a shambles, many items from the galley leaving their mark on the deck head. About 200 gallons of water entered the main cabin through the gap left by the top washboard of the cabin hatch. The cockpit was filled to the coamings.'

'When the knockdown occurred the boat was logging 8½ knots, which appeared all right at the time. I now consider that this was too fast and 7 knots would have been better. This was the speed at which we continued under storm jib afterwards.'

The following night *33 Export* was also badly hit. She had been racing neck and neck with *ADC Accutrac* since they crossed tracks off the Falklands a week before, and they must have been within a few miles of each other when, on 26 January, it again blew up after a period of gales alternating with near calms. It was blowing very hard when those who were to take the middle watch got ready below; the cabin of *33 Export* is so restricted that dressing for the deck in a rough sea would have taken all night for anyone less accustomed to it than her crew. Sylvie Delinondes takes up the story.

'At a quarter to midnight I went up on deck and Alain told us to put on our harness. The boat was sailing under the small heavy spinnaker. The wind was aft, the sea was on the quarter but with very big waves. From time to time two or three waves arrived at different angles but the boat held its course well and all seemed to be going fine.

Suddenly we heard a tremendous noise of water approaching and a huge wave coming from abeam started to crash down on us. The boat was not thrown on her side but the crest of the wave crashed across her decks, carrying with it the crew members who were sitting to windward as well as the helmsman. The helmsman found himself in the scuppers, one of the crew in the after-cockpit, and Eric found himself over the side except for a leg jammed between the lee rail and the life raft. We hurried to get him out of this position but his leg was completely twisted. He had broken the femur. We made a stretcher and installed him in it down below.'

A message that a crew member of *33 Export* had a broken leg reached Rio the following morning, but it was some hours before this was confirmed and reported to the Race Committee. Admiral Steiner immediately asked *G.B.II* by radio to pass messages to *33 Export* via any yacht, and contact was quickly established. *33 Export* explained that Eric Letrosne had a broken thigh bone and there was danger of secondary shock. The yacht was heading for Rio at about 6 knots.

Admiral Steiner had also contacted the Brazilian Navy and requested it to organise assistance. It was quickly arranged through the French tanker *Limousin* that the Japanese tanker *Wagasubira Maru* be requested to land the man at the nearest port. *G.B.II* was kept busy passing rescue messages, and ashore the Race Committee, represented by Admiral Steiner, Mike Jones and John Fox, were operating at full alert.

Next morning *33 Export* reported her position as 550 miles from Rio; the injured man was on pain-killers but required shore hospital treatment and perhaps oxygen. A message was then passed to all yachts:—

'Race Control has been in touch with Brazilian Navy at highest level, who have stated that all coastguard services in South Atlantic are attempting to find nearest vessel. At present best contact is Japanese *Wagasubisa Maru*. No confirmation that Japanese vessel has responded. Brazilian Navy state that range of *33 Export* from coast makes assistance by ship or helicopter ineffective. Negotiations with Brazilian Navy continue.'

An hour later Admiral Steiner radioed to *Tielsa* that the latest reports indicated she was the nearest yacht. As *Tielsa* had a doctor onboard, the injured man could be better off in her, and it was suggested that she should rendezvous with *33 Export*.

However Alain Gabbay in *33 Export*, whose thumb had been broken in the accident, felt that a rendezvous with any other yacht was not the solution as the injured man needed to be onboard a much bigger and faster vessel than any of the yachts. The Brazilian Navy at first reported that a tug was proceeding out from Rio Grande, 400 miles away, but later it reported that another tug was being deployed from Florianopolis instead; it turned out that this one was locked in by a wrecked freighter, although this was not known until the following day.

By Saturday evening Alain Gabbay decided to turn for Rio Grande, the nearest port, but still 400 miles away. It must have seemed onboard that no ship was taking much notice of their plight and the voice had a note of desperate urgency when her message 'Any ship come in please', was broadcast on the distress frequency. No ship replied, but immediately

Japy-Hermes, here seen at the start off Portsmouth, answered the distress call from *33 Export*.

Race Control answered with the latest situation.

On Sunday afternoon still no tug had sailed, but the Brazilian Air Force reported that a helicopter with a maximum outward range of 120 miles was standing by at Rio Grande. By this time *Japy-Hermes*, running under spinnaker before a fresh sou'westerly wind, was closing on *33 Export*, which recorded that the half gale of the morning was easing.

It was remarkably good navigation by both yachts that their rendezvous was made without delay. Yet the swell still running made it quite impracticable to transfer the injured man, and it was even too much for the doctor to be transferred by rubber dinghy.

This did not deter Jean Louis Sabarly, who courageously jumped into the sea, and swam through the waves to be dragged aboard *33 Export*. He must have felt quite at home onboard her, having raced as one of her crew to Cape Town. Eric Letrosne, the injured man, was also part of her crew then, and as a medical student would have had a good deal in common with Dr. Sabarly.

Certainly Dr. Sabarly's swim to the rescue set a standard that will ever be remembered with pride by ocean racers the world over. It was particularly suitable that the trophy for outstanding seamanship, presented by the Shipwrecked Mariners' Society, should be awarded to *Japy-Hermes* for this rescue.

On Tuesday, 31 January, reconnaisance aircraft of the Brazilian Air Force guided to *33 Export* a helicopter carrying an air surgeon. However Dr. Sabarly judged that a transfer to the helicopter would be too dangerous for his patient, so she sailed on and safely landed Eric Letrosne in Rio Grande, where his mother had arrived to supervise his quick transfer to hospital in Rio de Janeiro.

By then the rest of *33 Export*'s crew were in rather poor physical shape, with many abscesses, apparently caused by a virus infection. The small yacht club in Rio Grande did everything to help, and a doctor member joined her for the voyage to Rio de Janeiro, where she arrived a week later with the crew recovered and in cheerful spirits.

Going back to the day after the accident to *33 Export*, Eric Tabarly, by then in Rio, had assisted by contacting in France Madame Letrosne, and had given her the information that enabled her to rush out to Rio Grande.

Eric had sailed *Pen Duick* in to finish well ahead of the fleet. She had sailed outside the Falkland Islands and kept well out to the eastwards. This was a longer course than the rest of the fleet, which passed westwards of the Falklands, yet she increased the lead over *G.B.II* which she gained by Cape Horn; from then on she logged only one gale, compared with the succession of them experienced by the yachts that came after her, all on courses further to the west.

We last read of *G.B.II* on 24 January when she was 580 miles from Rio, catching up on *Pen Duick*, which had run into light headwinds, and *G.B.II* seemed all set to reach the finish a day ahead of *Heath's Condor*. Instead she ran into a frustrating period as her damaged mast track made the mainsail set badly when sailing hard on the wind. 'Damn calms. Fleet catching up,' logged Robert James with 300 miles to go; while *Heath's Condor* brought the breeze up with her. At noon on 27 January *G.B.II* still had 200 miles to go, and *Heath's Condor* had only six miles less. 'What a finish in prospect', logged *Heath's Condor* as the wind freshened and she could just lay her course. Then just after midnight there was a crash as her main halyard parted, due to chafe and wear. Quickly the topping-lift was improvised to get the mainsail in business again, but she must have lost distance from this.

Come the dawn, *G.B.II* was in sight from *Heath's Condor* for the first time since leaving New Zealand. She was to windward and very slightly ahead. Then came the sight of land, and not long after that the race to the finish was over. *G.B.II* crossed the line just 18 minutes ahead of her to gain well-earned line honours

Kings Legend approaches Rio with the Sugar Loaf ahead.

for the leg, to balance those of *Heath's Condor* in the second leg, and in the first leg *Flyer*, who reached Rio only 12 hours behind, and therefore easily led the two leaders on handicap; *Flyer* had missed the calms which had plagued them, but her crew might well have prayed that the calms come back to check the speeds of the low handicap yachts not far astern, especially *Gauloises II* and *Traite de Rome*.

It was not calms so much as headwinds which slowed the approach of the next three; but they came into a fighting finish just three days after the leaders. First of them to cross the line was *Kings Legend*, ten minutes later *Disque D'Or*, and 65 minutes after that came *Tielsa*. This gave another handsome supplement to *Flyer* to add to her previous lead of only 40 minutes from *Kings Legend* for the first half of the course round the world. *Gauloises II* was believed to be less than a hundred miles off at 4 p.m. 31 January, and had until 10.24 next

morning to cover it; this would make her almost certain to win the leg as *Traite de Rome* had by then little chance of finishing in time to beat her; *Adventure* had no chance at all, while all the others had to give *Gauloises II* time on handicap.

Before then *ADC Accutrac* arrived at 6 p.m. The wind had died as she approached the coast, but Clare Francis and her crew had sailed a fine race to put her in the top third of the fleet and to beat *Kings Legend*.

Then, in the quiet hours of the night, a light was seen approaching. It was *Gauloises II*; she crossed the line at 3.24 a.m. local time to win the leg on handicap. Perhaps this could be some consolation for Eric Tarbarly, her owner, because his outstanding achievement as skipper of *Pen Duick VI* could not be accepted for the official race results. In any case it was a superb performance by Eric Loizeau and his crew.

128

10 Rio at Carnival Time

Six weeks at sea, confined to the limitations of a yacht so tiny compared with the vast loneliness of the Southern Ocean, gave a compelling urge to reach harbour again. Eve Bonham of *ADC Accutrac* told how 'We spent the first three weeks at sea talking about Auckland, and the next three looking forward to Rio'.

For those who arrived in daylight, Rio first appeared as a great white city against a background of green mountains. As they sailed closer the Corcovado statue of Christ the Redeemer showed up above it as though floating in the sky. Then closer and glamorous beaches traced gleaming lines beside the sea.

The race finish was off Ipanema, one of the most inviting beaches, while the actual line was made by two towers on the Pta do Arpoador.

Once across this line each yacht sailed past Copacabana Beach, perhaps the most famous of all Rio's beaches, then on past Sugar Loaf, an extraordinary conical rock 1,200 ft. high, and into her berth off the Iate Clube do Rio de Janeiro. This is an exclusive Brazilian club of which membership is most sought after, and very expensive too; air-conditioned restaurants, bars, saunas, barbers—everything is there. There is also an enormous swimming pool but, before diving in, each member or visitor has first to visit the club's medical centre for a foot inspection and clearance permit.

Sailing is just one section of the club's activities. In addition, many of the members own fast and commodious power craft, besides many more smaller craft, with deep sea fishing

a very popular sport. The club's facilities for maintaining these craft are good, with two slips, workshops, chandlery and excellent storage hangars. It also has an inner boat harbour of its own, but this is too shallow for round-the-world yachts, so these were berthed on the outer wall, with stern anchors holding them off. Sheltered except in strong southeasterly winds it is a lovely situation near to the mouth of the harbour, flanked on the southern side by the Sugar Loaf, with beyond it Copacabana and Ipanema beaches. Then on the other side is Rio City, with the Corcovado Statue of Christ rising over 2,000 ft. behind it.

The club had just finished running Laser championships, and would have the World Soling Championship after the Round-the-World fleet had left; so the Vice-Commodore, Senor Alberto Ravazzano, and Admiral Roberto Monmerat, the Director of Sailing, were kept very busy.

The Club's own maintenance facilities were not designed to cope with such a visitation from big sailing yachts of the round-the-world fleet, but splendid support was given by the Brazilian Navy which was again friendly and helpful at all levels, thanks to Contre-Admiral Hugo Schieck. What is more, the yachts' repair budgets, which in many cases were getting very slim by this time, suffered no further exhaustion from repair work in the naval dockyard.

Philip Jenkins was kept busy organising the club's support for the yachts; assisting him to arrange hosts for each yacht was Margaret Travis, whose husband Frank Travis and also

Don Rendall scrutinized the yachts' equipment before they sailed. The Race Committee from England was provided with an office within the club close to the yacht berths, where Admiral Steiner, Mike Jones and John Fox were well assisted by Maria Joao, Beth Young and Edna Bueno, who between them knew who did what in Rio and where they might be found. John Anderson, with his perfect knowledge of Brazilian, was a tower of strength and thoroughly deserved his berth in *Flyer* for the last leg.

A particular asset for the race organisation was the club's own radio station, which could contact yachts before they arrived. Actually the first to come in, *Pen Duick VI*, beat the organisation as Eric Tabarly found better winds on his approach than anyone expected ashore. He was welcomed at his berth off the Club by Admiral Steiner, and congratulated on an excellent passage from New Zealand. He had already been told by radio that it had not been possible to confirm his entry in the race as his rating certificate was invalid; however, he was invited to sail back with the Fleet to Portsmouth, where he would be warmly welcomed by the Race Committee and given the same facilities as the competitors.

Admiral Steiner also gave Eric Tabarly a short letter, putting it on paper, and Eric answered it promptly; it was a warm and generous reply, worth recording; so here is a translation of the French text.

'Dear Admiral,

In reply to letter dated 3rd February, I fully understand the reasons which have led your Committee to exclude *Pen Duick VI* from the Round the World Race, since you cannot overrule the ORC's decision. I am grateful for your kind offer to accompany the fleet to Portsmouth as a non-competitor. Unfortunately the lack of competition cannot create sufficient interest to pursue that leg and I intend therefore to return to France.'

Yours sincerely

Eric Tabarly

The yachts berthed off the Iate Clube do Rio de Janeiro, with the Sugar Loaf standing guard above them.

We have seen already how *G.B.II* and *Heath's Condor* duelled for the first to finish, with a matter of minutes between them. Within three days of that, half the fleet had finished and their crews were enjoying the comforts of the Club and the glamour of Rio, greatly enhanced by the city's famous Carnival, which

Prize giving in Rio. Left to right, Ian Coombes of *Long John* whisky, Admiral Roberto Monmerat, Director of sailing, Admiral Ravazzano, Vice-Commodore of the Iate Clube do Rio de Janeiro, 'Otto' Steiner and Peter Siemson of the Race Committee at Rio.

coincided with the fleet's stop-over. Most of the crews danced all night at some time in the Carnival parades; some recovered in time to visit other parts of Brazil, and were perhaps surprised to discover that it is a country bigger in size than the U.S.A. Bus rides seemed almost too exciting; 'Broaching off Cape Horn was child's play compared with one bus I went in', narrated Eve Bonham, speaking at a pace to match the bus's progress.

Nearly all were back in time for a memorable prize-giving at the club, which presented superb prizes for the leg from Auckland. A piper from British Caledonia Airways played the guests in with appropriate Scottish tunes; then a Samba band and dancers performed in clothes more suitable for a temperature in the 100's. Everyone joined in the dancing, and the swimming pool nearby provided alternative exercise.

The festivities over, or mostly over, came the usual rush of work to prepare for leaving, with scrutineering, clearing essential replacement gear from the Customs, and Immigration formalities, besides storing and provisioning, the latter much helped by Molly Jenkins.

It had been the intention to start in two groups, those below 65 ft. length overall starting 48 hours before the larger yachts; this would increase the chance that they would all arrive at Portsmouth within a fairly short period, and be there together for longer before disappearing to their home ports. This had been the method in the first Whitbread Round-the-World Race four years before, and had proved effective, as the early arrivals had to wait for only a few days to see their slower-sailing friends of seven months competition; some of these slower yachts turned out to be ahead on handicap of early arrivals.

Until Carnival time the weather this year proved settled and predictable so that, as long as the two separate starts were at the same time of day, similar starting conditions might be expected for each. Then the weather changed and a succession of cold fronts succeeded one another, bringing unsettled weather with rain and thunderstorms, sunny and overcast days all mixed together; a longish period with no wind at all would be followed by another with fresh breezes. The weather pattern meant that either group might have the misfortune to be becalmed near the start whereas the other group might have a fresh breeze.

This made the Race Committee reconsider the starting arrangements. With the overall positions so close right down the fleet, many of the skippers were unhappy about the pursuit type of start under the prevailing weather conditions. In any case the fleet had proved very much closer in speed than in the first Whitbread race; in each leg the interval between first and last had been only about five days, except for those which had suffered some accident and perhaps been forced into an intermediate harbour.

Thus the sailing instructions were amended to delay the start of the smaller yachts by 48 hours. This meant that all would start together at 2 p.m. local time on Wednesday 22 February.

After this new starting plan had been published there was a sudden fear that it would have to be changed again. Rumour reached the club that gunnery exercises at sea would prevent the fleet leaving the bay; it was only a rumour, but the Race Committee visualised the situation if the yachts sailed out to the gunfire, uncertain whether it was a parting salute or a bombardment. Saturday afternoon is tradi-

Start of the final leg in Rio Bay.

132

tionally a time for rumours to spread, but contacts with the Brazilian Military authorities were well established and, though at the weekend, it was quickly confirmed that the start would not be hindered by gunfire.

The eve of the start was thoroughly hot, as no wind stirred the bay. Wednesday morning looked as though the pattern might be repeated as Philip Jenkins, chairman of the race committee from the Iate Clube do Rio de Janeiro, gathered his team to conduct the start, assisted by midshipmen from the Brazilian Naval Academy. The line was inside the bay, between Farolette de Villegagnon Light and a buoy moored off it.

Even as the fleet left their berths a light breeze filled in from the south which gave a perfect windward start; the yachts reacted to it as though they were class racers, so close were most of the yachts to the line as the gun fired.

Yet once more it was *G.B.II* that had the best of it.

Eric Tabarly waited until all were over the line before he took *Pen Duick* across, having after all decided to accept the invitation of the Race Committee to sail with the fleet. He had also requested to go through the same scrutineering procedure as the others beforehand, showing that even the most experienced of ocean seamen loses nothing by having such a careful check of safety equipment.

Within an hour the whole fleet had cleared Rio Bay and disappeared to the west. 'Course. From the starting line to Portsmouth, England' read the race instructions, and the handicap distance was given as 5,500 miles. This was more than a thousand miles shorter than any other leg of the race. Yet still no mean distance for any race.

11 The Final Leg Home

This final leg, although the shortest, could be expected to give a wide variety of conditions. Off the Brazilian coast in late February a monsoon pushes out into the south-east trades of the South Atlantic. It gives hot and sticky conditions, with a good deal of rain and variable winds, generally north of east. About 800 miles northwards of Rio, around Recife, the monsoon is usually pushed back to the coast by the south-east trades, which give pleasant conditions with the wind abaft the beam.

The south-east trades, averaging force 4 in early March, would give moderately fast reaching up to the doldrums, which would probably be met about 2° north of the equator as a belt parallel to it and perhaps only 100 miles across.

Then would come the north-east trades, blowing at their strongest in March to give two thousands miles of sailing in reasonable conditions but hard on the wind. After that, approaching the Azores, would probably come the biggest problem of that leg. Just as the South Atlantic High was a major obstacle in the first leg from Portsmouth to Cape Town, so also the Azores High would almost certainly be a vital factor in the race results of this final leg from Rio to Portsmouth.

After the High would come the area of westerlies, although easterly headwinds are quite common there in March. By then the yachts would be in their final run of some 1,300 miles to the finish, but it would be no time to relax. It is often a surprise that statistics show a higher gale frequency in the North Atlantic mid-winter even than Cape Horn in its mid-winter. It would be well past mid-winter when the yachts reached the area of westerlies, but the vernal equinox is traditionally a time for gales; they probably would not be so severe as the worst of the Southern Ocean storms, and certainly would not be so cold. But the nights would be much longer than in the Southern Ocean summer; there would be plentiful shipping to avoid, and, once in the English Channel, tidal stream running against a gale would give much steeper seas than in open ocean storms.

As the yachts cleared the thermal breezes in Rio Bay following the start, the weather was at first light enough for all to regain their sea legs. 'A general feeling of relief to be off on the final leg home', logged *Heath's Condor*, skippered this time by Robin Knox-Johnston, with Leslie Williams remaining aboard in support. Again a new crew had taken over *Adventure*, continuing the Armed Forces policy of spreading experience of this great venture among as many sailors, soldiers and airmen as possible; this time Lt. Col. Robin Duchesne was in command.

All the other yachts had the same skippers, but there were several crew changes; indeed *ADC Accutrac* was the only competitor which had her entire crew unchanged all the way round the world, which surely says much for the leadership of Clare Francis, besides her ability to pick a compatible crew in the first place.

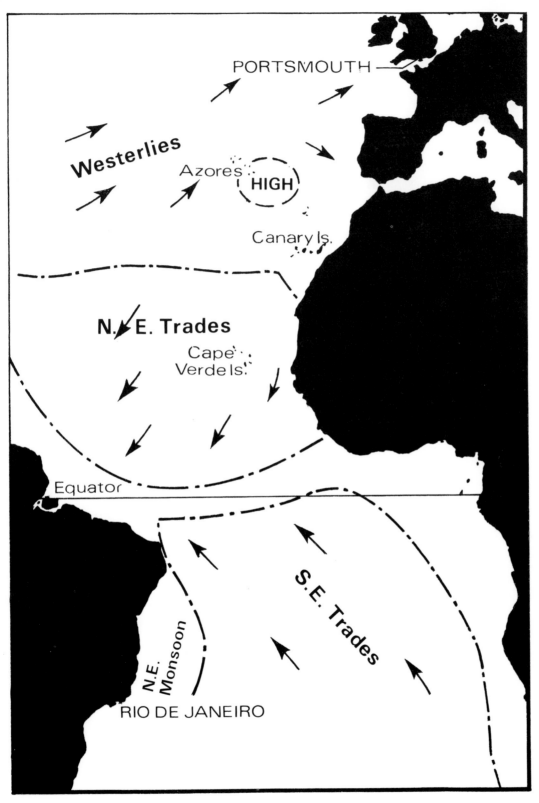

PORTSMOUTH

Westerlies

Azores

HIGH

Canary Is.

N. E. Trades

Cape
Verde Is.

Equator

S.E. Trades

N.E.
Monsoon

RIO DE JANEIRO

Crew compatibility is certainly one of the most important factors in such a long and demanding race; good food is another. Both these factors were to be severely tested in the first few days out of Rio as progress was slow, the heat unpleasant, while 'flu germs from Rio seemed to have stowed away in several yachts. 'Very hot and sticky for sleeping below. Our straw mats helped', logged *Adventure* on 26 February when the cooking schedule was altered to avoid the midday heat. *ADC Accutrac* caught a four-foot barracuda to help the lunch menu, but Bumble had 'flu and the fresh vegetables were going rotten after only two days.

Heath's Condor also had problems with her fresh provisions. After five days it was found that the egg boxes bought in Rio were infested with maggots. Robin Knox-Johnston ordered a massive clean out, followed by fumigation of the after cabin, which was done by burning polystyrene. The log read, 'Result–blackened aft cabin including clothing and bedding. Jules (who lives there) was not amused'. Nor were several other members of the crew who imagined they were suffering from styrene poisoning.

Flyer's concern was to get the fresh meat frozen when the air and sea temperatures were so high. The second day out the main electric fuse blew, and the engine had to be run for long hours to get down the deep freeze temperature; but this in turn added to the heat in the boat.

Generally the fleet remained in close company for several days, with frequent sightings. On 28 February, *G.B.II* was just in the lead, followed by *Heath's Condor*, for whom dawn broke to show *Pen Duick* one mile away on the quarter 'breathing down our necks, and it is obvious that we can attain no more boat speed than her in these conditions', logged *Heath's Condor*. It was squally at times, with periods of continuous rain; the double bang of a Concorde airliner passing high overhead seemed to jar the nerves of the crew.

That same day *Adventure*'s crew had an anxious time when her forestay fitting failed, leaving her mast in some danger. The wind was no more than moderate at the time, so the fracture may have started in her knock-down soon after rounding Cape Horn. Improvised repairs took $3\frac{1}{2}$ hours, but without a sufficiently powerful wrench for the job they did not prove up to the strain, as next day they gave way with the wind no more than light. She was held up a further 2 hours for repairs as the vice used to compress the ferrule broke and the skipper had to decide whether or not to turn into Recife, 250 miles away, for more permanent repairs. He decided to sail on, and this time the crew's improvisation stood up to several thousand miles with some thoroughly tough sailing.

Once within the influence of the south-east trades proper, all the yachts made excellent progress, mostly selecting courses that gave good speed combined with a reasonable gain to the eastwards, which would put them to windward when they came to the north-east trades. Thus on 2 March *Heath's Condor* set a course of 45° to the apparent wind, altering the compass course as the true wind varied between east and east-south-east.

At noon that day, she was to windward and a few miles ahead of both *G.B.II* and *Pen Duick*. Strictly *Pen Duick* was not entered in the race, but to all the leading yachts the well known racing ability of both yacht and skipper made her the trial horse they strove to beat.

Following these three maxi-yachts on 2 March came *Flyer*, then *Disque D'Or*, so close that she was best placed of all on handicap; yet there were only fractional differences between these two, as well as *Traite de Rome, ADC Accutrac* and *Gauloises II*.

Heath's Condor and *G.B.II* both met the doldrums on 4 March about 150 miles north of the equator. It was when tacking into the lightest of winds that *G.B.II* ripped her mainsail just as she sighted *Heath's Condor* with the coming of dawn; it took four hours to repair the sail and by that time *Heath's Condor* was pulling ahead. However, neither of these two dropped below 100 miles in the 24 hours they took to get through the doldrums, and this must have cheered them until they heard that *Pen Duick*, only 65 miles to the west of them, shot through the doldrums to gain 100 miles on them.

In the next batch *Flyer* followed on almost precisely the same track as *Pen Duick*; yet a day later the conditions were quite different. 'Hit the doldrums at 2°30′ north—heavy rain— numerous squalls but with little wind', she logged and in 24 hours covered 85 miles compared with 197 miles by *Pen Duick*.

There was an amazing difference in the treatment served out to yachts quite close together in the doldrums; *Adventure* suffered as much as *Flyer*, while *Neptune* and *33 Export* came out relatively well. It did not seem to depend upon the longitude, nor even upon the time at which different yachts hit the doldrum belt; if luck was not the major factor, then certain boats and crews showed superiority in those special conditions. As they came into the

north-east trades from the doldrums, *Neptune* and *33 Export* had pushed forward to be best placed on handicap, *Traite de Rome* was still in third position; *Flyer* and *Kings Legend* had dropped well down the list.

Next came some two thousand miles sailing hard on the wind into the north-east trades at their strongest; indeed their March average is twice the strength of that in October. Thus on 6 March *Heath's Condor* was sailing close-hauled with two reefs in the mainsail and the No. 2 genoa, which had not been used in all the previous legs. The weather was fine, not too hot for sunbathing, while the remaining rotten eggs and potatoes were cleared out from below. 'Life onboard is very pleasant, though a little dull', recorded Gerard Dijkstra in *Flyer* which, even after her difficult crossing of the dold-rums, was so far ahead on handicap for the whole race around the world that the best strategy would surely be to keep out of trouble and avoid any extremes. *Kings Legend*, her rival for the overall trophy, had done even

In the monsoon conditions off Rio keeping cool was quite a problem for the cook of *Kings Legend*.

worse in the doldrums, while both *Traite de Rome* and *Disque D'Or* would have to catch up several days on her to win overall.

The north-east trades were far from steady. In 15° north, just about the centre of their area, Eric Tabarly ran into a private doldrum for nine hours; 'Temps de pot au noir', he recorded but still lost very little distance to *G.B.II*. When *ADC Accutrac* reached almost the identical position three days later, on 11 March, her mainsail blew out, and after four hours for repair was re-hoisted with three reefs; yet she still covered over 200 miles to windward that day, with the wind up to force 7 and the sea quite heavy. 'Very busy for deck crew', she logged and the sail repairers had little time for sleep. At this stage *ADC Accutrac* had caught up extremely well after her mediocre doldrum crossing and on handicap was best placed of all the fleet for the final leg, with a clear advantage over *Neptune*, which lay next.

These calculations inevitably depend upon the positions logged by each yacht, and in the trade wind zone the skies are usually clear enough for ample sights of sun and stars to allow accuracy in navigation. In cloudy conditions, the positions must often be estimated, and sometimes yachts within two or three miles of each other by sighting, recorded positions as much as 20 miles apart. Thus earlier in the race *Pen Duick* recorded *Disque D'Or* in sight four miles astern in overcast conditions, when their reported positions differed by some 20 miles. 'Je ne sais pas qui a raison', logged Eric Tabarly, and if he did not know who was right, it is quite reasonable for any other yacht's navigator, with the same limitation of equipment, to be uncertain of his position at times.

By 11 March *Flyer* was taking special interest in the position and movement of the Azores High, although it was still 1,000 miles away. It was well developed, with a pressure of 1037 mb, and appeared to be north of the Azores moving in a north-easterly direction. She was receiving the reports from Lisbon, and some felt she had a special advantage by having

Flyer's navigation and communication centre is a model of functional layout and was specially important to strategy.

onboard an instrument which automatically translated radio morse code into letters and figures. Her navigator had time to comment on the striking absence of bird life that day. The trades were strong, blowing at force 6/7, with squalls up to 40 knots. *Disque D'Or*, 35 miles ahead of *Flyer* at that time logged squalls of over 40 knots with an average wind force 7.

Tielsa, 140 miles behind *Flyer* on 11 March, was making excellent speed with the trades although, when at their strongest, she had to lower her mizzen for repairs, and rig a jury lower shroud when a strand in the wire rigging parted. In five days of these brisk trade winds she covered 1,093 miles—60 miles further than *Flyer*, which was sailing closer to the wind.

Debenhams, on 11 March, ran into a little private doldrum in mid-trade area, just as *Pen*

Duick had done three days before. With no wind at all she twice turned through 360°, before the wind came again; next day it was strong enough for a keel bolt to work loose, which meant that the bilges needed pumping out every hour.

Japy-Hermes found much to comment upon in the trades, including whales, turtles, porpoises, passing ships, and a butane gas container which she proclaimed as a danger to navigation.

On 14 March *Pen Duick* looked all set for showing the way to the finish once again, even if not eligible for official entry into the race. She was 200 miles south of the Azores, still holding a light breeze; *G.B.II* was 100 miles further away from the finish, although slightly to windward, while *Heath's Condor* was 130 miles behind *Pen Duick* and well to the westward, which was to leeward in the prevailing conditions.

Then the easterlies began to fail, and in the next 24 hours *Pen Duick* covered only 81 miles, as though to make up for the fact that she did so well in the doldrums. *G.B.II* closed up on her, but next day her barometer showed she was right in the Azores High, which seemed to be an oblong with its longer axis stretching across their path.

G.B.II never completely lost the wind, but tacked frequently as it varied in direction, her crew working hard to make the best of the conditions. On 16 March, while still some 100 miles short of the Azores, she sighted *Pen Duick* six miles on the port bow, and it must have been thoroughly thwarting for the crew of *Pen Duick* to see her there.

Neither knew where *Heath's Condor* was at this time, which must have been just as well for their peace of mind. Robin Knox-Johnston had correctly assessed that the High was not moving to the east as forecast, so he planned to sail round to the west of it. In the early hours of 15 March she was barely moving at all on a beautiful starlit night. 'Got the doc up and out on a spinnaker pole for pictures', Robin wrote,

and went on to describe puckishly how they tested the watertightness of his boots by lowering the pole. At noon her daily run was a reasonable 127 miles, almost the same as *G.B.II*'s and much better than *Pen Duick*'s. Then came the slightest drop in her very high barometer reading, and that evening a halo round the moon gave added hope that they might be getting clear of the High.

Yet the wind still remained very light, sometimes with no more than little catspaws which were not enough to move the masthead windvane; to help this Peter Blake went aloft and used Bovril as an improvised dampening fluid. The crew tended to be irritable, fearing that *G.B.II* might be doing better, 150 miles to the east. She wasn't and actually this was *Heath's Condor*'s winning day, with a run of 50 miles better than *G.B.II*. *Heath's Condor* still had another 24 hours of very light airs, but the look of the weather was changing and with the morning of 17 March the zephyrs were coming out of the south-west. This enabled her to steer a course between Flores and Fayal, which at noon was in sight far away to starboard.

At that time both *Pen Duick* and *G.B.II*, 16 miles to the east of her and actually 70 miles closer to Portsmouth than *Heath's Condor*, were both in sight of San Miguel; but another day was to pass before either of them felt any westerly wind, and both were utterly becalmed during much of this time.

G.B.II suffered more damage in those calms than in many a previous gale, or was it that strains may have accumulated throughout the race to make things more vulnerable? She was rolling to a swell, with no wind at all to steady her, when three spinnakers in quick succession were torn, but soon repaired. Then came more serious damage when the main boom broke in two, and this was not repaired before the end of the race.

Meantime the second batch had run into the High. First *Disque D'Or*, and almost level with her came *Flyer*, then *ADC Accutrac* and *Tielsa*, in the same latitude as *Flyer* but to the west of

John Roberts keeps a close watch on the sail trim in *Kings Legend* when bright sunshine became the helmsman's problem, instead of cold spray.

her and in sight of each other; *Kings Legend*, which was to the south-east of them was actually closest to Portsmouth of the bunch. 'We had a hopeless day', logged *Flyer*, who was puzzled at the position of the High given by radio from Monsanto, as it had moved very fast since the previous report.

Tielsa covered a miserable 57 miles in the next 24 hours, while the others logged between 85 and 90. On 18 March *Flyer* had worked out that the Azores High had an almost windless area some 300 miles north and south by 450 miles east and west; this had been more or less steady for the last six days, but the extreme high centre had moved around within it. She recorded that only *Gauloises* was trying to sail around to the west, but none of them knew that *Heath's Condor* had already done so, and that day she made 193 miles in steady westerlies.

There was certainly no reason why *Heath's Condor* should disclose to those astern that she had found a way round the High; so she kept radio silence until required to report her position by the race rules.

Meantime *Gauloises* was keeping well to the west, and was not to lose the wind at all, although in the early hours of 19 March it veered from south-east to south-west without dropping below 15 knots, as she hurried on her way close to Flores. By 19 March *G.B.II* was also getting clear of the High, but *Heath's Condor* had got clean away from her and was also just ahead of *Pen Duick*.

Disque D'Or had come through the High fairly well and had gained a position to lead *Flyer* by 100 miles on 21 March, compared with being level with her just before they met the calms.

Heath's Condor was the first to pick up the strong westerlies after the Azores High, and this gave her really fast sailing back to England.

Each following yacht in her turn had really light conditions in the Azores High, except for *Gauloises* which went round it. Worst hit was *Neptune*; she covered only 23 miles in the day's run to noon 19 March; next day, with the wind breathing hesitatingly from the west, she sailed no more than 62 miles. The effect of this vast area of high pressure was to bunch the fleet, but as each got clear of the calms the distances opened out again when they picked up strong westerlies.

These gave *Heath's Condor* easily her best three day runs of the leg, sailing almost as far as her best three days in the Southern Ocean storms. The yawing motion as big seas rolled up around her caused concern over her steering, as the aft bulkhead showed signs of being too weak to bear the strains of the steering box secured to it; this meant crawling into the lazarette to shore up the bulkhead with timber, wedges and stanchions, backed with a few prayers that this would last out for the final three days of the race.

On 20 March she reckoned to be 47 miles ahead of *Pen Duick* and 130 miles ahead of *G.B.II*, so morale was high. Yet by the next day some were beginning to suffer from lack of sleep due to constant calls for all hands to change sails. On such a fast run-in to the finish it is a matter of fine judgement by the skipper how much he can drive the crew; a sprint of all-out effort put in too early may leave the crew exhausted before the finish. It may even go further than that, as there could be real danger in making a landfall with poor visibility in a gale on a lee shore, should the crew be unable to react quickly.

At 3 p.m. 21 March *Heath's Condor* was

sighted by an R.A.F. Nimrod aircraft some 270 miles from Land's End. Excitement became intense ashore as the news was broadcast on radio and television. The battery of telephones in the Race Control office at Portsmouth were in almost continuous use as relations, friends, acquaintances, the Press and those just thrilled by the whole adventure rang through to ask the latest positions of each yacht. 'Shall I catch the next plane from Copenhagen,' someone asked, 'or will there be time for me to wait until tomorrow?' Inevitably there were numerous callers from France and many wanted more details than the dictated messages of the latest known positions.

There were also many Press calls from Holland, with *Flyer* so well placed for the overall win. Yet it was far from all over yet. A routine check aloft on *Flyer*'s mast disclosed that the runner tangs had broken; they were replaced with wire strops round the feet of the spreaders and all was well. Yet had this not been noticed before a gale struck her two days later, she could even have lost her mainmast.

Next day, 21 March, *Flyer* recorded another end-of-race problem when it was found that her tanks had 360 litres of fresh water less than expected; she had enough left to cover the 1,000 miles left to Portsmouth if it was a fast passage; but if anything went wrong, she might have to call somewhere else or even ask for outside help, which would imperil her race position.

However, she might expect a fast passage to the finish as a particularly deep depression was forming in the Atlantic with a whole brood of other ones forming up behind it.

Heath's Condor felt the first of this tough weather that night when in her second gale since the Azores the steering box again worked loose. She was sailing extremely fast, particularly when surfing, as once more repairs were improvised in the lazarette. In the morning the wind eased to fresh so she changed from her gale spinnaker to a bigger one, yet with the afternoon the next gale was blowing up, and all hands were called to hand the spinnaker. At 9 p.m. Robin Knox-Johnston logged 'Sailing too fast for safety' and a storm jib was set with the wind gusting to 60 knots. 'The seas in the Channel are far more dangerous than anything seen in the Southern Ocean, and steering is restricted to experienced helmsmen'.

The fact is that when a westerly gale is blowing against a strong ebb tide in the English Channel, the seas become much steeper than in an open ocean gale of the same strength. The storm varied between force 9 and force 10 during the early hours of 23 March as *Heath's Condor* stampeded up the Channel.

Visibility was good and at 3 a.m. the loom of a light was sighted away to the north. It was Portland Bill lighthouse, and three hours later she set a stay sail on squaring up for the Needles Channel, then the gale spinnaker off Hurst Castle at breakfast time; but everyone onboard was far too excited for breakfast, and most had gone without sleep the night before.

Television, radio and Press men jostled for the best positions at the finish; the wind dropped to a modest strong breeze, so some ventured out in the Press boats with a reasonable chance of their equipment not being ruined by the spray. They were close alongside to photograph the crew of *Heath's Condor* in action as they handed the gale spinnaker, and set a bigger one. Soon afterwards the wash of a passing craft set up a most unwelcome roll, so television viewers saw her spinnaker blow out right in front of the camera.

Worse was to come a few minutes later. The race instructions for the finish off Southsea beach stated that Elbow Spit buoy had to be passed to port, so *Heath's Condor* headed for the buoy shown on her chart as Elbow Spit. When she reached it, she found it had another name marked on it, so she gybed to look for the right one and in doing so ripped her mainsail. The mistake was that the buoy had been renamed since the race started and this had not been made know to the competitors. She was told of this by a committee boat, and the seven

Robin Knox-Johnston, celebrates line honours at Portsmouth for *Heath's Condor*, supported by his wife and daughter.

minutes lost in this search were subtracted.

At once she turned back to make the correct finish under headsail alone. For the second time she had won line honours, and also had the private satisfaction that this time she had won the unofficial race with *Pen Duick*.

Yet *Pen Duick* was not far behind and 3½ hours later she crossed the line after the race committee had met her off Cowes to inform her of the change in buoy names, in case the radio message to this effect had not got through in time. *Pen Duick* was not an official entry, as she had not the valid rating certificate required to make her eligible; but she had been invited to cruise with the race and was assured that she would receive the same privileges as those racing. Thus her finish was marked with the

same gun as the others, and following *Heath's Condor* she was directed to a special berth in H.M.S. *Vernon* in the creek reserved for the racing yachts.

The gale had eased to a fresh breeze by the time *G.B.II* crossed the finish line soon after midnight, but it was still cold and wet as she came to her berth in H.M.S. *Vernon*'s creek. Yet this did not stop a strong turn-out of friends and supporters, who welcomed her crew with vigorous enthusiasm. Well they might, as *G.B.II* had made easily the fastest elapsed time for the whole race; it came to 134 days, which was within hours of breaking the record for the fastest time sailing round the world, already held by *G.B.II*. Few well-informed yachtsmen before the start would

Nick Ratcliff at the wheel of *Kings Legend* as a committee boat closes on her in the West Solent.

have backed *G.B.II* to finish the course anywhere near the leaders, with her crew made up from those with enough enthusiasm to raise £4,000 each for the venture; the success brings the greatest credit to all these very genuine amateurs, but the outstanding leadership of Robert James, their skipper, brings him into the very front rank of long distance racing yachtsmen. There was a double cause of celebration for him, as soon after arrival he heard that his wife, sailing alone round the world behind them, had safely rounded Cape Horn and reached the Falkland Islands.

Easter Saturday was the sort of day that kept most holiday makers at home, but quite a crowd braved the rain and wind to visit H.M.S. *Vernon* and look with wonder at the three yachts home. These were the maxi-yachts, but to most visitors they looked small indeed to venture round Cape Horn; they found it hard to believe that *Great Britain*'s amateur crew had actually sailed round the world faster than the best time ever achieved by the professional crews of the great clipper ships.

The persisting strong westerly winds were

(Left) *Disque D'Or* sails fast up the Solent with the chimneys of Portsmouth in sight.

bringing along the remainder of the fleet at fine speed. At dawn on Easter Sunday *Disque D'Or* was reported at the Needles, and the line judges took up their post on Southsea Front. She was across the line to a fine finish when most people would be still toying with their eggs for Easter breakfast. This put her well ahead on handicap of those already finished, and well in the running for a place on this leg to add to her excellent record of two fourths and a fifth in the previous legs. So much for the suggestion before the start that Swiss dinghy sailors would be out of their depth in the Southern Ocean!

Pierre Fehlmann, skipper of *Disque D'Or*, came into the Press Office beside the yachts and was told how long the different low handicap yachts had to go if they were to beat him on handicap, both for the leg and for the whole race. He could win the leg if *Gauloises* took another two days and *Traite de Rome* took about 3 days, but Race Control had worked out to the minute when either of these had to finish to beat her. Third place between her and *Traite de Rome* for the whole race was still in doubt, even assuming that *Flyer* and *Kings Legend* finished shortly.

Both these two were shaping up for yet another close finish between them. At Cape

145

Flyer gives a demonstration of how hard she was sailed. Left, she starts to broach; centre, her blooper drags in the water, and right, its sheet lets go under the strain and lets her come upright again so the sail flies out ahead.

Town *Flyer* had won by two hours, at Auckland *Kings Legend* beat her by 73 minutes, and the latest reports suggested that they were coming up the Channel neck and neck.

Around mid-day *Kings Legend* was reported in the Needles Channel. She was sailing very fast before half a gale, and temporarily seemed to get out of control as she made a Chinese gybe, allstanding, in the Hurst Narrows. Those watching with anxiety from the Needles had no sooner seen her settle down under a poled-out genoa with a couple of reefs in the mainsail, than they sighted another yacht sailing into the steep seas on the Bridge, so called as it is a relatively shallow ledge across the entrance to the Needles Channel. It was *Flyer*, and she was rolling wildly under a big spinnaker, which blew out as they watched.

By then a committee boat had met *Kings Legend* off Lymington, and then turned on to join a pair of powerful motor launches with Dutch supporters waiting off Hurst Castle for *Flyer*. Onboard the committee boat with me was Rod Stephens, a famous yachtsman himself and also a partner with his brother Olin in the American firm of Sparkman and Stephens which had designed both these two yachts; indeed it was to turn out that the five yachts in

the race from the design firm were to win the first five places on handicap for the whole race.

Flyer was sailing under blast reacher and blooper with a full mainsail as we closed in for Press shots of the skipper at the wheel. 'Sorry you weren't here for your birthday yesterday, Corny,' I hailed. 'Hope to finish for my son's today', he replied, and the finish line was only 12 miles ahead.

A squall overtook us, laden with hail, and the blooper let go in a broach to blow loose until lowered by her crew. 'She's still got a lot of sail up', said Robert Stephens as she sailed more upright, but just as fast. The wind had increased to a full gale, and as we sped along at 15 knots, the wind was overtaking us at about 25 miles an hour. The spring tide pushing against the gale kept it rough enough in the Solent to make steering difficult.

Approaching Southsea, we could see that the Front was lined with cars, in spite of the hail and wind. *Flyer* had taken a couple of reefs in her mainsail, and after rounding a buoy would have only some 400 yards to sail, beam on to the wind, before crossing the line about an hour behind *Kings Legend*.

Yet just as she reached that buoy a squall hurtled down on her at 55 knots, and would

Captain Mike O'Kelly R.N. and Admiral 'Otto' Steiner congratulate Cornelius van Rietschoten onboard *Flyer* as she berths in H.M.S. *Vernon*'s creek. Captain Dudley Norman on the left with head down.

have knocked her down with that amount of sail if she turned onto the final course. Down came the blast reacher, and the mainsail was partly lowered to take in another reef. In this state she stalled, heeling well over, but lying stopped in the water.

The line judges watched horrified as the squall drove her sideways towards the beach. Quite big waves were breaking on it, and if once she touched there would surely be no chance of getting off without outside help. She might even be severely damaged before help could get to her. There was a nightmare thought of the yacht wrecked only 200 yards from the finish when victory seemed certain after sailing 27,000 miles round the world.

When the lee-shore rocks seemed almost beside her, a small jib shot up the forestay. At once *Flyer* picked up her heels and belted close-hauled over the finish line.

An Easter afternoon crowd of several thousand waiting to greet her in H.M.S. *Vernon* had been spared the anxiety of this sensational finish. Yet her arrival was dramatic enough on its own account. *Flyer* was certain of the overall win, and there was no more popular skipper in the fleet than Cornelius van Rietschoten. He had planned his whole campaign with prodigious care, sailed his yacht with notable aplomb, and made good friends wherever he went. *Flyer* was his own private and unsponsored entry.

12 Back in Portsmouth

With *Flyer* home 78 minutes after *Kings Legend*, each had beaten the other twice in their own duel around the world and *Kings Legend* had taken 13 days off the time of her sister yacht *Sayula*, winner of the first race. However, *Flyer* was even 58 hours better, so she became confirmed as certain winner of the Whitbread trophy for the whole race. Yet second place overall was still open to *Traite de Rome* if she could finish within two days of *Kings Legend*. Both *Kings Legend* and *Flyer* were out of the running for the final leg win, as *Disque D'Or* had already bettered them; yet her position could still be challenged by either *Gauloises* or *Traite de Rome*. Neither was very far away, and the weather forecasts promised ample more wind to come.

That Easter Saturday afternoon, while *Flyer* caused a few missed heart beats in the 55 knot squall off the finish, it was blowing a strong gale—force 9—off Portland Bill. *ADC Accutrac* was having rough seas as she sighted the Bill, and lost half of her No 3 genoa as it ripped and fell over the side. Four hours later, at 8 p.m., she was hurtling up the Needles Channel in the dark under storm spinnaker and mainsail; it was blowing force 8 as she passed, but the moon shone through to add romance to the dramatic scene.

A couple of minutes before 10 p.m. she was safely across the line; surely the first woman skipper in history to sail her vessel around the world via Cape Horn. What a splendid race it had been for Clare Francis; her's was the only

crew to remain unchanged the whole way; her yacht had climbed steadily in race positions, with a ninth in the first leg, seventh in the second, fifth in the third, and she proved fifth for the race overall. Her seamanship had been exemplary and the yacht had suffered no real damage throughout all the severe trials of the race.

ADC Accutrac came quietly through the darkness to her berth, where a substantial crowd had gathered to greet her, in spite of the hour and the weather. She secured alongside efficiently, then suddenly euphoria burst as crew and welcomers flew into each other's arms amid screams of joy. Clare Francis stayed at the wheel, her husband beside her, both looking mildly astonished at such wild excitement.

The wind in the approaches had veered to north-west on Easter Sunday, 26 March, but it remained near gale force to give *Gauloises* one of her best 24 hour runs. At 4.35 p.m. local time, she crossed the line to become the leading yacht on handicap for leg 4. *Traite de Rome* might still beat her, but from her last signalled position this seemed unlikely; indeed it turned out that *Gauloises* was to repeat her victory in the leg to Rio, giving her two wins and a third place, although the loss of her rudder in the second leg put her down to sixth overall. This was a splendid performance by Eric Loizeau and his crew, sailing the oldest yacht in the fleet; it was also a great credit to Eric Tabarly, her designer and owner.

For Clare Francis the ordeal of a night interview by the Press offered variety from leading the crew of *ADC Accutrac* through a gale.

A busy night ahead was promised for the team of race organisers handling the finish, with two more yachts known to be approaching, and the position of à third uncertain as a figure seemed to have been corrupted in her last signalled position.

The wind had veered back to west and increased to full gale force once more as *Tielsa* came through the Needles Channel about an hour before midnight, and finished just over two hours later. Whatever time of day or night a yacht came into the creek in H.M.S. *Vernon*, first on board to welcome her in was Admiral Steiner, chairman of the race committee, accompanied by Captain Mike O'Kelly to bear the official naval welcome on return to his establishment from which they had set out. Other members of the race committee followed

onboard about half a jump behind to ensure that each member of the crew was welcomed personally and that enough champagne was provided for all to celebrate their achievement. Relatives, friends and the Press followed onboard very soon afterwards; but on cold, wet nights the whole bunch of crew and welcomers were soon led to a warm shed immediately beside the creek where a hot meal of grilled steaks was awaiting the crew, with ample beer for the supporters as they gathered round the table to exchange news.

Tielsa's crew had scarcely finished their steaks when *33 Export* was seen coming in. Unlike the others she had sailed round to the south of the Isle of Wight, and had gone unnoticed in the rain as she passed Bembridge, to finish 54 minutes behind *Tielsa*. This was to give her fourth place for the leg; she had won the second leg, but overall dropped well down in the order as in each of the other two legs she had been forced to turn into intermediate harbours. Alain Galbay and his crew had worked very hard indeed to achieve this successful result; a great deal had to be done on the boat at each stop to get her fit for the next leg, and their living conditions onboard were the most austere of all.

'You seem to have learnt quite a bit of English since the race started, Alain', I mentioned as we spoke together after *33 Export* came in, and Alain suggested with a smile that he had needed to know what the other yachts were doing from the radio chat.

Moored in the creek, right amongst the yachts, was Peter Richardson's motor fishing vessel *Unknown*, again acting as committee boat. The reception committee returned to her cabin awaiting the next call, as there would be no time for bed that night. An urgent message came through as we prepared our loads of champagne and beer to greet the incoming yacht. It was dead low tide with the dockside far above us. 'Come on the sherpas', said Captain Mike O'Kelly R.N., as he led with his load up a vertical ladder, round the head of the creek in the dark, and down another ladder to the pontoon where the yacht was to berth.

It was *Neptune* coming from the Bembridge direction. The wind was down to force 6, strong breeze, as she crossed the line at about 6.30 a.m. local time. It would be steak breakfast for her crew. *Neptune* was eighth overall, and had placed consistently around this in each leg; she had sailed a thoroughly competent and seamanlike race with very little going wrong throughout the 27,000 miles. Her elapsed time for the whole race, on a rather longer course than the first Whitbread, was some four hours faster than the winner of that race. She was in quite splendid condition at the finish, and Bernard Deguy with his crew had every reason to feel fully satisfied with their achievement.

By breakfast time on Easter Monday *Gaul-*

oises was established as the leg winner. *Traite de Rome* had not finished in time to beat her; but the wind remained fresh to strong and she crossed the line that evening in time to gain second place for the leg, pushing back *Disque D'Or* to third by over three hours. It meant two second places, a third and a fifth to give *Traite de Rome* third place overall, which was a superb achievement for Philippe Hanin and his multinational crew, which in different legs had come from all nine E.E.C. countries. Her arrival in the dark was greeted by many representatives of the European Communities Commission, besides a strong gathering of the crew's personal friends, coming from many countries.

Another 24 hours was to go by, but still the westerly winds kept up their strength for a batch of three fighting it out in the approaches. Indeed at midday it was again blowing at gale force at Portland Bill to let *Japy-Hermes* finish up with her fastest day's run of the leg. She came through the Needles Channel in the dark, driven by gusts of up to 40 knots and reached the finish before midnight. *Japy-Hermes* had the build more of a splendid fast cruiser than an out-and-out racer, so her aim was a good reliable performance, and this is just what Jimmy Viant and his crew achieved. The accent was on youth, and at 26 Jimmy had successfully skippered his boat and crew around the world in quite splendid time. No wonder his father was proud when he greeted Jimmy at Portsmouth; Andre Viant had skippered *Grand Louis* into third place overall in the previous Whitbread, and Jimmy had been in his crew.

Less than an hour later came a really close finish. At Auckland *B & B Italia* had beaten *Debenhams* to the line by a matter of seconds; off Southsea *B & B Italia* was beaten to the finish by 3 minutes, but this time it was *Adventure*, which on handicap put her eighth for the leg. She was the same *Adventure* that in the first Whitbread had won three of the legs to be second overall, but this time she was 4 days faster in spite of the longer course, to gain seventh overall, showing how much faster was this race than the first.

B & B Italia was in ninth place overall; Corrado di Majo and his crew had sailed a good race having overcome all the problems, including gale damage that at one time made it seem that he would be forced into Hobart.

By the next day, 29 March, some of the early finishers were beginning to leave for their home countries. Often the crews of those staying in the creek would rush up on deck to cheer the yacht setting out, and many were the promises to meet again at the final prizegiving. This had been announced for 26 June in London's historic Mansion House, with His Royal Highness Prince Michael of Kent making the presentations; it would be followed by a mammoth party at Whitbread's London brewery nearby.

The miserable weather, with scarcely a sign of sunshine but persistent strong wind and ample rain, did not prevent those first days after the finish being a period of almost constant euphoria. Rounding of the Horn, a complete circumnavigation, a terrific welcome, no cold night watches or sudden calls for all hands on deck—all made life seem extra good. Apart from friends and relatives of the crews, more than ten thousand members of the general public paid a fee for naval charities to come into H.M.S. *Vernon* and see all the yachts at close quarters; when the crews visited their pubs nearby they were received as heroes.

Already the race stories were becoming sprinkled with plans for the next one. 'It was that Irish whiskey in the porridge on St Patrick's day, that stopped the met. forecast, or we'd have beaten *Kings Legend* for second overall', suggested one of the crew of *Traite de Rome*. 'No way,' answered a *Kings Legend* man, 'if we had not run out of beer before the Azores High, we would have beaten *Flyer* overall.' 'I'm going for lighter displacement in a New Zealand entry next time,' insisted Peter Blake, mate of *Heath's Condor*. 'Let's keep the same course,' was a constantly recurring comment to members of the race committee, with the assumption that we would run another race in four years; but some suggested a start about two weeks later to give shorter nights on the tough second leg.

In the early hours of 30 March, and only a week after *Heath's Condor* finished for line honours, *Debenhams* crossed the line to bring the whole fleet safely home. On handicap for the overall result she placed 13 out of the 15, yet her time would have put her in third place in the original Whitbread race; but silver trophies were not really the objective for the Ridgways. 'I'm thrilled to be back,' Marie Christine told me, holding the hand of her 10 year old daughter Rebecca, 'but I would not have missed it for anything.' 'For me,' said John Ridgway, the virtuoso of high adventure,' this voyage around the world produced all I could wish for.'

Appendix 1 MATERIAL AND EQUIPMENT

Prepared by: Captain J. A. Hans Hamilton, RN
CEng., FIMechE., MIMar E.
Captain M. A. Jones, MVO RN CEng.,
MIMechE., MIEE.
Lieutenant Commander R. Q. F. Evans, RN

Qui desiderat Pacem praeparet bellum
(Let him who desires peace, prepare for war)
Vegetius

More aptly we should say, 'if you are planning for success in a hazardous adventure, be prepared to combat disaster'. Lord Montgomery upheld that the greatest single factor in the success of any venture is 'the MAN'. This is certainly true of the Whitbread Round the World Race. In numerous cases man has made up for shortfalls and, as will be seen, a number of failures in this race would have remained so without man's ingenuity and skill under pressure. Even so, care in design, installation and use of equipment is a precursor which must meet safety and survival requirements and provide the means to complete the venture. Many spin-off benefits accrue from the development of the design of yacht equipment suitable for use in a trans-ocean race and the Whitbread/R.N.S.A. four yearly event has done much to accelerate advances in certain fields, particularly those of safety and reliability. It was remarkably apparent, even to the casual observer, that the fleet of Round the World Race yachts in the creek at H.M.S. *Vernon* in August 1977 was better equipped and prepared for the competition ahead, by a whole order of magnitude, compared to their counterparts who left four years before in 1973 for the first ever full-crewed yacht race round the world.

Before man can take charge and perform to his best, the boat must be planned and built. There are specific areas of investigation in a study of material and equipment for him to use which are:

(a) A detailed study of the requirement and the means to meet it.
(b) Study of the conditions through which equipment would be subjected and cycled.
(c) The application of a systems approach to design and installation of equipment to meet those conditions.
(d) Consideration of reliability, maintainability and availability, coupled with further consideration for spare parts, jury-rigs, extremes of temperature, moisture, humidity and excessive wear.
(e) Material strengths, their physical properties particularly their durability and cost.

Looking at the first of the items above, one must state an aim or aims before starting to build or convert a yacht for a race of such length and duration. We assume three aims: to finish, to finish fast, and to finish first in that order. To achieve these aims the boat and crew must first survive, in order to push the boat to her limits.

The sea has always been hostile, and is likely to remain so. Survival of the boat is one problem, survival of the crew in the event of total loss of the yacht is another. Progress has been made by national and international bodies to encourage yachtsmen to be conscious of and to face up to realities. Besides meeting the requirements for safety equipment laid down by the race regulations, all yachts had their own survival routines worked out, and were subject to inspection at each port of departure.

Requirements for survival in the event of total loss of the yacht are: liferaft capacity for the whole crew: survival clothing for each crew member: first aid kit: emergency rations and water: emergency transmitter and receiver: the means to deploy all the above very quickly.

Medical opinion has stated that in the Southern Ocean, below a latitude of 50°S, the body will freeze in under 10 minutes if seated upon the single skin of a liferaft commonly found in ocean racing and cruising yachts. Liferaft stowage therefore, must cater for the greater bulk of a double skinned liferaft for use in Antarctic waters together with either the integral or separately packed support equipment in space which is discreet, drainable and accessible. Without exception, yachts were fully prepared with emergency supplies and radios, although the means of deploying the equipment overside varied according to the size of the yacht, greater difficulty being found in the smaller ones.

Having catered for the means to finish, we move on to the means of finishing fast (and hopefully, first!) Speed is a function of 'pushability' and if the boat is to be pushed to the limit, it is no use having fittings and fastenings which are fined down for weight and strength to the point where normal working is near their strength limits. In very nearly all the yachts entered for the 1977/78 race, the size and strength of fittings were up to the task they were set, but this in itself presented problems in certain cases. The market for trans-world ocean racers is not vast, and the equipment of the size and type required is not available on every yacht chandler's shelf. The situation appears to have improved over the last four years and in general, suitable upper deck fittings, sheaves, tracks and winches are not only available, but are reliable and maintainable. Replacing them, using air freight and defraying customs duty, can easily double the initial cost of the item, as many owners found to their horror.

But everybody hopes to win, and the ul-timate pushability of the boat depends on the power house—mast, spars, rigging and sails. It is here that one is inevitably thrown back onto the strength of materials.

Unfortunately, the strength of materials is not the only factor to be taken into account. For the non-metallurgist it is sufficient to say that high strength materials invariably bring related problems, particularly those of brittleness, stress, corrosion and fatigue. High strength stainless steel is particularly prone to these adverse properties, and can be affected by a combination of time (age) and the number of times that stress is applied or removed. One of the common uses of stainless steel is in rigging where, for strength to withstand the enormous forces, say, those acting on a lower shroud when the yacht is attempting by its own stability to withstand a 'knock down' gust, the size would be unacceptable in anything but stainless steel either in rod or multi-strand form. The rigging of a yacht for this race could be paramount to all other strength considerations. Investigation of failures in both the 1973/74 and 1977/78 races gives support to the belief that without a much greater attention to inspection and replacement, particularly of lower shrouds and mainstays, the faster pace in the 1981 race might well result in more power house losses.

In 1973/74, many questions were asked about the strength and reliability of stainless steel rigging and to the critics the manufacturers quoted 'X' years of experience without failures. However, the replies did not carry too much comfort when it was shown that by the time a yacht had completed its tuning and training and had sailed from Portsmouth to the Antipodes, it had sailed in distance and cycled, in terms of stress reversals, the equivalent of seven years of normal ocean racing. This time put the knowledge on certain materials on the threshold of experience. Material failures, such as that recorded in photograph 1, occur where constant chafe or contact by other agents on a stainless steel surface combine with conditions where the steel member is subject to stress cycling or reversal. The action takes place when the natural protective coating that normally builds up on a stainless steel surface is prevented from forming.

Salt water, combined with stress, can cause a failure along the grain boundaries. This in turn leads to a fatigue failure. So, whilst stainless steel looks good, do not be fooled by its superficial appearance—it can have hidden horrors! The desire to finish fast naturally takes its toll on the material strength throughout the yacht's fit, and it rests upon the skipper to decide the optimum sail plan for all conditions. There does not seem much point in carrying more sail than that which produces

maximum hull speed, particularly where one could be faced with a knock-down. The transmitted stresses to the lower shrouds in this circumstance are enormous. Naval architectural sources have described the figures as almost incalculable with the present state of knowledge on maxi-length boats. There is plenty of scope for a systems approach to design in this vital area.

There have been sufficient instances of rigging failures and stranding, both in 1973/74 and 1977/78 to recommend replacement at least at the half-way point, and for competitors

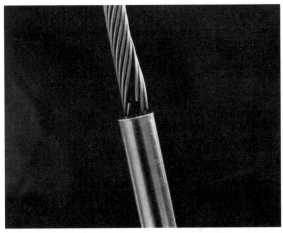

Photo 2 *33 Export*'s inner forestay. Four of the outer and two inner stainless strands parted at the swaged end fitting where there was considerable corrosion.

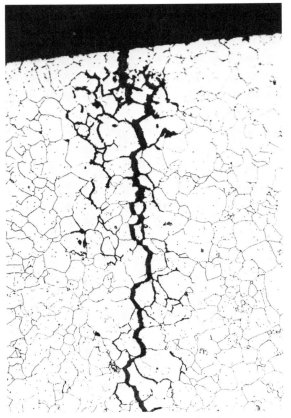

Photo 1 Start of a typical crack system showing essentially intergranular path of cracking (× 100).

Photo 3 *Adventure*'s forestay bottle screw lower end fitting fatigue failure. Fatigue in two phases, first from thread root to approximately 1/3rd. diameter, probably from knock-down to Rio. Second from 1/3rd. to 2/3rds. diameter from start of leg 3 to 6 days out from Rio.

Photo 4 *Flyer*'s starboard running backstay tangs. Fatigue originating from filed notches at lower left hand corners and progressed (conical markings) 90% through left section and 70% through right.

to plan in future to employ crack detection devices at every stop. Whilst under way, regular routine visual inspection is essential. (Photos 2, 3 and 4.)

Let us now turn to the failures of material and equipment experienced in this race. Without writing a separate book it is not possible to list them all; some of the more noteworthy from which lessons may be learned have been picked out. They fall into groups according to the severity of the effects and the first concerns those which hazarded a yacht's progress in the race.

Heath's Condor lost her G.R.P. and carbon fibre mast on the first leg. It was a new departure in mast making and had not had the

degree of proving which more conventional spars have received. This lack of proving was particularly significant in view of the late modification to the rigging, which had been set up less than 12 hours before the start. The change of rudder by *Gauloises II* in Cape Town as an expedient was to turn against her, since it later transpired that she would have been better to have kept her original rudder, probably resulting in a high final placing. On the third leg, *Adventure* sprung a leak in a gale five days out of Auckland; it occurred through two cracks in the G.R.P. where the trailing edge of the keel faired into the bilge. The pumping rate to stem the inflow increased throughout the remainder of the leg, with considerable variation according to weather conditions—200 pumps/hour in calm to over 1,000 in bad weather. Conditions never became critical but it was a worry to the crew who did not know how far things would deteriorate. The fault lay where the original trim tabs had been glassed in. The two Whale pumps (aluminium casting) survived this semi-continuous use to Rio, the three Henderson pumps (plastic) did not.

Material failures varied from manufacturing faults as in the shattering of two identical winch barrel castings in *Debenhams* to the use of the wrong material such as the plastic sheaves in blocks from *Tielsa*; these failed in the Southern Ocean, possibly because they became brittle in the low temperature. In the case of *Debenhams*'s winches visual examination, without destructive testing and metallurgical examination under microscope, appeared to suggest the use of faulty castings in the original assembly. Production line crack detection methods could have avoided these failures which in themselves might have caused serious injury to personnel. In the event, they significantly impaired the crew's safe sail handling ability on both Roaring Forties legs of the race. (Photo 5.)

Tufnol sided blocks seemed particularly prone to tearing or shattering when coming across stays, halyards or tracks. *ADC Accutrac*

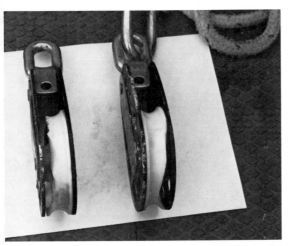

Photo 5 Two failed sheaves from *Tielsa*, the material probably became brittle at low temperature.

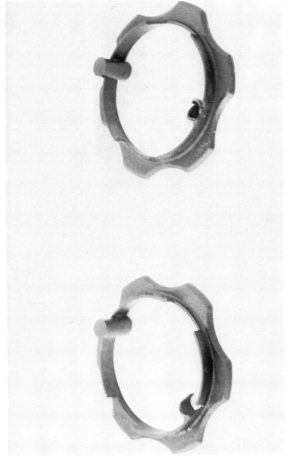

Photo 6 Two broken plastic rings from *ADC Accutrac*'s winches. Both spring loaded plunger posts have failed.

and *Kings Legend*'s 3-speed automatic winches gave problems which probably stemmed from the design stage. Despite regular maintenance, *Accutrac* had repeated trouble from the plastic closing ring on the top cap assembly which broke in two places. (Photo 6.)

Adventure's steering gear gave trouble which was aggravated by the inaccessibility of the

Photo 7 *Tielsa*'s spinnaker snap shackles. failure on overload has occurred at the left of the pin joint.

Photo 8 *Tielsa*'s starboard aft coffee grinder. The top lip of the self tailing gear failed with a corresponding crack in the lower plate.

157

assembly for repair and maintenance. Instances of overload failures were abundant such as on *Tielsa*'s spinnaker gear (Photo 7) and her starboard aft coffee grinder top lip. (Photo 8.)

Traite de Rome's masthead spinnaker halyard gantrys were adequately adapted in Auckland using U bolts attached to the remaining stubs. These served her well, although they showed signs of 'walking through' the light alloy webs. (Photo 9.)

G.B.II's boom broke on the last leg three days out from Portsmouth in very light winds, the failure occurred at the slot cut for the foot tensioner sheaves probably because of the restraint of a canvas band rigged to the preventer in a heavy rolling condition. (Photo 10.)

An interesting example of life limit failure was *Adventure*'s starboard genoa block which failed on a training sail off Cape Town prior to the start of the second leg. This block had been round the world in the previous race and examination of the stainless steel swivel pin revealed a fatigue fracture propagating from the bottom of the keep pin hole failing in bending rather than shear. Renewal of these pins after say, 10,000 miles sailed would be prudent, bearing in mind that the block and sheave contained by them weigh 2 lbs. and could cause a terrible injury. (Photo 11.)

Needs must when the devil drives and there were many examples of the determination and ingenuity of repairs whilst under way. It was a sad discovery for *ADC Accutrac* who, having three times rewound the armature of the engine's starter motor, vital to charging the batteries, was only to discover the engine was seized! The rewiring was meticulously done using wires from the stereo speakers, insulated with a tight bound layer of tape to keep the diameter down, and taking three days for each job. The steering reduction gearbox in *Heath's Condor* gradually broke away from its bulkhead mounting. On the last leg it was effectively stabilized by shoring up with an assortment of

Photo 9 *Traite de Rome*'s mast cap. Both spinnaker halyard gantries had failed. U bolt jury rig is beginning to walk through the vertical gantry webs.

Photo 10 *G.B.II*'s broken main boom. The fracture had taken a path through the set screw holes.

gear. (Photo 13). *33 Export*'s crew made a most effective repair to her main boom on the second leg by cutting out buttstraps from an aluminium watertight door and contouring them to fit. (Photo 12). This, highlights the need for

Photo 11 Stainless steel swivel pin from *Adventure*'s genoa sheet block. Concoidal fatigue markings start at bottom corners of keep pin hole. Note hole drilled off centre.

Photo 12 Repairs to *33 Export*'s main boom utilising plate cut from an aluminium bulkhead door. (Right) mounting. (Below)

Photo 13 Emergency shoring in *Condor*'s after compartment to stabilise the steering gearbox and the bulkhead mounting.

unceasing planned routine inspection of all gear. A near disaster for *Flyer* was avoided when the running backstay tangs were found cracked and near to failure on the last leg. (Photo 4) Prevention is better than cure, and there was clear evidence in all yachts that this was the rule. The fact that they all finished the race is this evidence.

We mentioned earlier a 'systems' approach to design and installation of equipment as part of an overall planned 'purchase and fit' rather than a bringing together of what's on the shelf. Boats which were most trouble-free had this strategy applied, and we feel this to be right for a race of this kind. Systems which lend themselves to this treatment are:—

Communications—Transmitters, receivers, aerials, standby and emergency arrangements, and radio hazards.

Propulsion (ex sails) and Power Generation—starting, charging, power consumption, stand-by and emergency arrangements for power generation.

Galley—fittings and support including: victuals, diet, food, stowage and rationing.

Fuel—for all uses: propulsing, power generating and cooking. Problems of mixing a variety of fuels: diesel, petrol, gases and paraffin.

Water—storage, distribution and consumption monitoring.

Electrical Power Distribution—breaker and control panel system, susceptibility to water damage, upper and belowdeck fittings, consumption capacity and spare parts.

Steering Gear—design principle, inherent strength, failure potential, emergency steering, weakest links, feasibility of repair and emergency procedures.

Ship's Plumbing—all forms of piping, both fixed and flexible for fresh and salt water: ship's side skin fittings, cocks, taps, drains including cockpit drains.

Damage Control—watertight compartments, collision control, flooding, pumps for all purposes. Fire fighting. Survivability of hull.

As an example, it is worth a look at radio communications in this race where the systems approach spelt out a tangible contribution to *Flyer*'s success. In all seagoing communication centres we have seen, her installation is a model. Its functional layout and equipment was provided to meet a carefully studied and accurately assessed requirement right down to the on-line morse decoder for receiving weather forecasts.

In the main, radio communication was good and its contribution to safety and morale cannot be overstressed. Notable failures were confined to those yachts which had been seduced away from well tested and tried marine radio equipment, by the lure of the 'the latest' in the belief that it must therefore be 'the best'. The only sure guarantee is reliability based on proven satisfactory performance in use over a period and under conditions similar to those in which the equipment will be used.

Yachts using fully tunable synthesisers, notably *Heath's Condor* and *Kings Legend* in identical equipments, suffered much inconvenience and in the case of *Heath's Condor*, some delay from unreliable equipment. Two quite different reports came from *ADC Accutrac* and *Flyer*, where there equipment remained serviceable at all times and was easy to operate. Clare Francis would have preferred a synthesiser if a proven one had been available, but her sponsorship relied upon radio communication, so she could not afford to take risks and her Marconi Falcon II did all for her that she needed. *Flyer* and *Tielsa* were fitted with Beker Sirius 400's and the clarity and brevity of their procedures was to be commended. Some operators failed to observe the golden rule that a powerful transmitter can blot out the weak, perhaps emergency, transmission of the small man. Radio communication is a means of passing messages, not for holding conversations.

A word on radio hazards. In the small installations found on yachts not fitted with radar, radio hazards are reduced to those which:

(a) can be a danger to personnel—radio frequency burns.

(b) can damage or affect the performance of electrical equipment.

In almost all yachts, radio hazards had received little or no serious attention. Yet when questioned about the possibility of crew grabbing hold of the stay which was transmitting 400 watts of power, 'Yes', they had and did take precautions. It seems to us that these were less rigid than the possible dangers warranted. Next, when asked about the effects on instruments, 'Oh, yes! They did seem to be affected, some of them, particularly the digital instruments'. We wonder if any examination has or will be made to see if the transitory effect of radio frequencies or radiated power on instruments has any permanent effect on any of the range of makes of instruments fitted in yachts.

Finally, it is worthy of note that few yachts were seriously delayed by a material failure for which no provision had been made or forecast. Most yachts, if closely inspected below, could be seen to be floating chandlery stores, workshops and miniature sail lofts. This gear was in excellent hands, and those to whom this race was a new adventure experienced a steep learning curve into material practices. We have visited them at all the stopping ports and seen the material and equipment, including the results of the limits to which they are used and stressed. We think, as a result, that there is an abundance of experience waiting to be drawn upon by the whole industry catering for racing yachts which, in turn, will become the lot of the designers of the next race's contenders. After all, the first five came from the same design stable!

Appendix II Yachts and Crews

Adventure

LOA | 55 feet
LWL | 39 feet 2 inches
Beam | 14 feet 5 inches
Draft | 8 feet 4 inches
Displacement | 17.77 tons
Yacht club | JSSC & RNSA
First launched | 1972
Designer | Raymond Wall
Builder | Camper & Nicholson

Leg 1
Sqn Ldr J. H. Watts R.A.F.
(Skipper)
CPO A. Malcolmson
Sqn Ldr G. H. Glasgow R.A.F.
Lt E. F. M. Searle R.N.
Capt J. Stanyer R.E.M.E.
Flt Lt R. S. Ryott R.A.F.
Capt P. Enzer R.E.
Sgt S. Hope W.R.A.C.
CY A. J. Farnes
Fl Lt A. K. Webster R.A.F.

Leg 2
S/Sgt D. A. Leslie
(Skipper)
Ch Tech A. R. Mills
Sgt J. A. Hearl R.A.F.
CPO D. Wise
Capt I. S. Leslie R.M.
PO A. E. Brown
Lt Cdr R. C. Caesley R.N.
Capt J. Kiszely Scots Guards
S/Sgt D. J. McGilp
Sgt I. G. Spilstead
Flt Lt R. S. Ryott R.A.F.

Leg 3
Cdr I. C. Bailey Willmot R.N.
(Skipper)
Capt J. M. Rayner R.E.
Flt Lt I. Miskelly R.A.F.
Capt A. R. Manton R.A.
Capt J. S. Moore R.A.C.
Lt N. M. C. Chambers R.N.
CPO A. J. Moore
CPO J. Giblett
Lt P. L-C. Walters R.N.
CPO J. S. Kay

Leg 4
Lt Col P. R. Duchesne O.B.E. R.A.
(Skipper)
Sub Lt S. R. Kirby R.N.
Capt S. G. Thompson R.A.M.C.
Flt Lt P. Mumford R.A.F.
PO C. M. Toner
CPO V. C. Morgan
CPO A. Ritchie
REM C. D. Vaughan
Lt Cdr M. W. Kemmis Betty R.N.
Capt M. G. Paterson R.E.
Capt B. C. Winfield R.A.

ADC Accutrac

LOA	64 feet 6 inches
LWL	47 feet
Beam	16 feet 4 inches
Draft	9 feet 2 inches
Displacement	25.6 tons
Yacht club	Sea View
First launched	1974
Designer	Sparkman & Stephens
Builder	Nautor

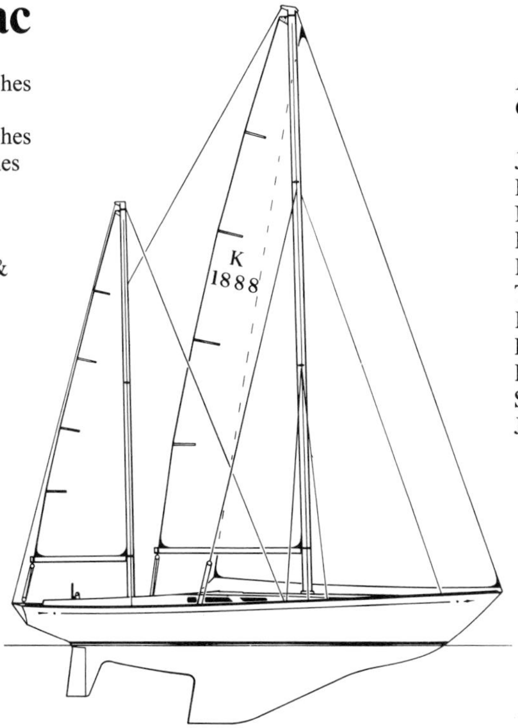

Round the World
Clare Francis
(Skipper)
Jaques Redon
Elizabeth Ogilvy-Wedderburn
Nicholas Milligan
Beat Gittinger
Robert Jackson
Tony Bertram
Robin Buchanan
Eve Bonham
Frederick Dovaston
Sam Badrick
John Tanner

B & B Italia

LOA	54 feet
LWL	43 feet 7 inches
Beam	15 feet 11 inches
Draft	7 feet 11 inches
Displacement	17.5 tons
Yacht club	
First launched	1972
Designer	Alan P. Gurney
Builder	Sangermans

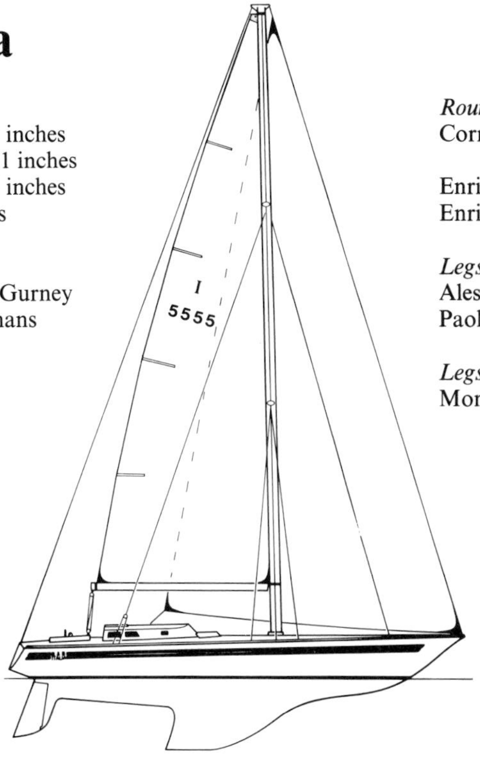

Round the World
Corrado di Majo
(Skipper)
Enrico Sala
Enrique Vidal Paz

Legs 1, 2, 3
Alessandro Quaglia
Paolo Martinoni

Legs 1, 3, 4
Monique Lattes

Legs 2, 4
Marco Facca

Legs 2, 3
Pierre Sicouri

Leg 1
Angelo Mezzanotte
Gianspirito Vocchelli
Enrico Francolini
Franco Bosia

Leg 2
Marina Pagani

Leg 3
Paolo Pozzolini
Vittorio Ferreri
Adriano di Majo

Leg 4
Julio Lattes
Ugo Dominici
Paolo Bartoli
Mariano Carrara

Debenhams

LOA	56 feet 1 inch
LWL	42 feet 6 inches
Beam	14 feet 8 inches
Draft	8 feet 4 inches
Displacement	18.43 tons
Yacht club	Ocean Cruising
First launched	1976
Designer	Holman & Pye
Builder	Seaglass Ltd

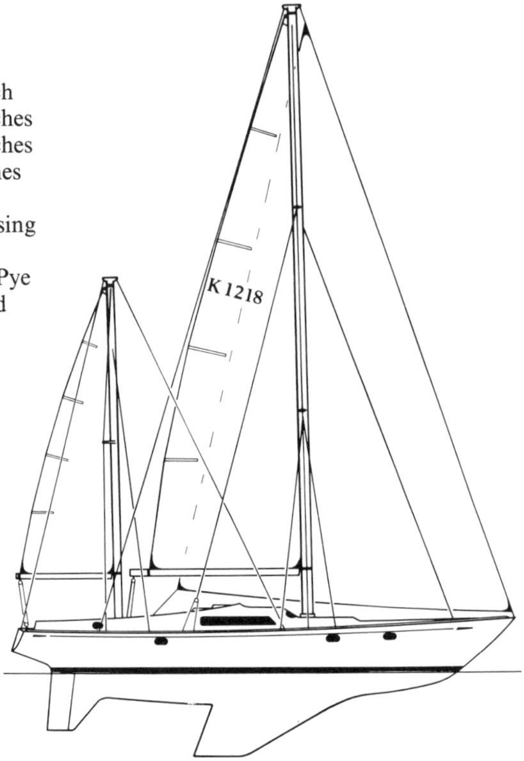

Round the World
John Ridgway
(Skipper)
Marie Christine Ridgway
Peter Brand
Roger Deakins
Dick McCann
Tony Dallimore
Colin Ladd
Stephen Lenartowicz
Noel Smart
John Covington

Legs 1, 2, 3
Robert Burns

Legs 1, 2
Alan Bose

Leg 2
Tom Woodfield

Leg 3
Alan Green
Chris Barker
Stafford Morse

Disque d'Or

LOA	64 feet 6 inches
LWL	47 feet
Beam	16 feet 4 inches
Draft	9 feet 2 inches
Displacement	25.6 tons
Yacht club	Swiss Ocean Racing
First launched	1973
Designer	Sparkman & Stephens
Builder	Nautor

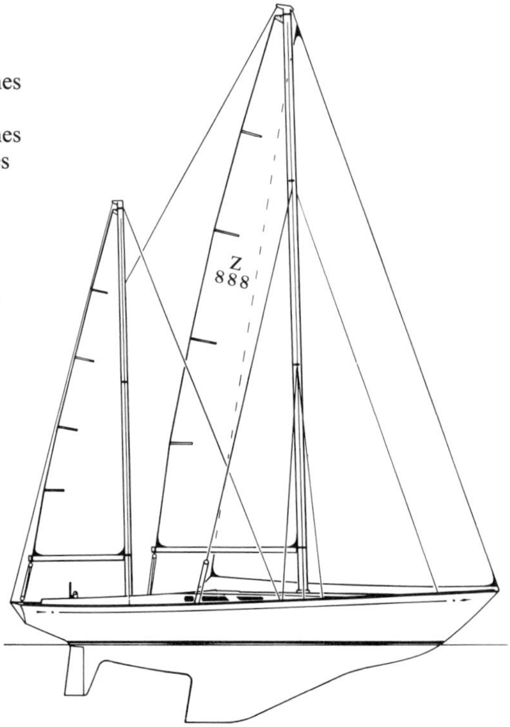

Round the World
Pierre Fehlmann
(Skipper)
Hans Bernhard
Donald Gautier
Alain Bussy
Didier Charton
Roderick van Schreven
Gerard Baudraz
Francis Reinhard
Philippe Cardis
Rene Blondel

Legs 2, 3, 4
Bruno Barde

Leg 1
Olivier Stern-Veyrin

Leg 2
Urs Eiholzer

Leg 4
William Stern-Veyrin

Flyer

LOA	65 feet 2 inches
LWL	49 feet 9 inches
Beam	16 feet 4 inches
Draft	10 feet
Displacement	24.6 tons
Yacht club	Kroninklijke Roeien Zeilvereniging 'De Maas'
First launched	1977
Designer	Sparkman & Stephens
Builder	Huisman-Vollenhove

Round the World
Cornelius van Rietschoten
(Skipper)
Marcel Laurin
Adrian Ford
William Johnson
Ari Steinberg
Christopher Moselen
Roderick White
Gerard Dijkstra
Hugh Wilson
Albert Dykema
Edgar Koekebakker

Legs 1, 2, 3
James Ashwood

Leg 4
John Anderson

Gauloises II

LOA	56 feet 8 inches
LWL	48 feet 9 inches
Beam	13 feet 8 inches
Draft	8 feet 11 inches
Displacement	13.4 tons
Yacht club	Société Nautique la Trinité
First launched	1967
Designer	Eric Tabarly
Builder	La Perrière

Round the World
Eric Loizeau
(Skipper)
Michel Guez
Alain Labbe
Francois Brillant
Alain Provost

Legs 1, 2, 3
Vincent Gazeau

Legs 2, 3, 4
Philippe Soetaert

Legs 2, 3
Patrice Carpentier
Loic Caradec

Leg 1
Jean Pierre Labbe
Nicolas Loday

Leg 4
Thierry Norman
Francis Freon

Great Britain II

LOA	77 feet 2 inches
LWL	68 feet 2 inches
Beam	18 feet 5 inches
Draft	9 feet
Displacement	32.58 tons
Yacht club	Royal Southern
First launched	1973
Designer	Alan P. Gurney
Builder	D. Kelsall, Sandwich Marine

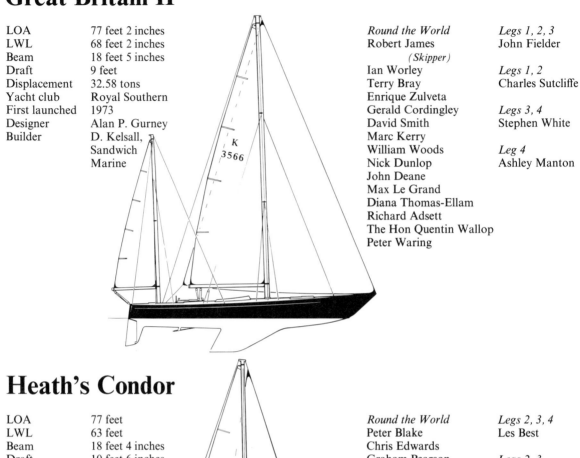

Round the World	*Legs 1, 2, 3*
Robert James	John Fielder
(Skipper)	
Ian Worley	*Legs 1, 2*
Terry Bray	Charles Sutcliffe
Enrique Zulveta	
Gerald Cordingley	*Legs 3, 4*
David Smith	Stephen White
Marc Kerry	
William Woods	*Leg 4*
Nick Dunlop	Ashley Manton
John Deane	
Max Le Grand	
Diana Thomas-Ellam	
Richard Adsett	
The Hon Quentin Wallop	
Peter Waring	

Heath's Condor

LOA	77 feet
LWL	63 feet
Beam	18 feet 4 inches
Draft	10 feet 6 inches
Displacement	40 tons
Yacht club	RNSA
First launched	1977
Designer	John Sharp
Builder	Bowmans

Round the World	*Legs 2, 3, 4*
Peter Blake	Les Best
Chris Edwards	
Graham Pearson	*Legs 2, 3*
David Dickson	F. Buchanan
Justin Smart	
Julian Gildersleeve	*Legs 3, 4*
Graham Carpenter	Allan Prior
Paul Newell	
Herman Vanura	*Leg 1*
	Andrew Cully
Legs 1, 3, 4	Jack Kehoe
Leslie Williams	John Carter
(Skipper 1, 3)	
	Leg 2
Legs 2, 4	Rorrie Roos
Robin Knox-Johnston	W. Abram
(Skipper 2, 4)	
	Leg 3
Legs 1, 2, 3	Peter Visick
David Alan-Williams	Roddy Coleman
	Leg 4
	Ianto Jones

Japy-Hermes

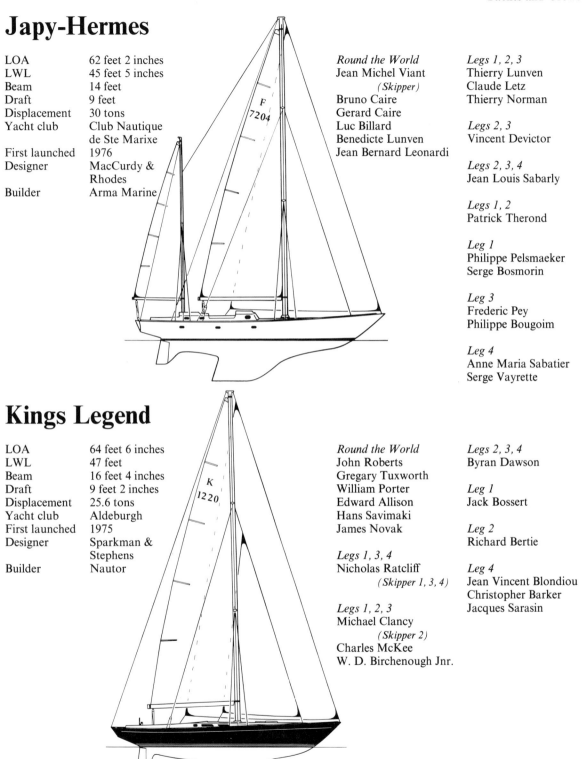

LOA	62 feet 2 inches
LWL	45 feet 5 inches
Beam	14 feet
Draft	9 feet
Displacement	30 tons
Yacht club	Club Nautique de Ste Marixe
First launched	1976
Designer	MacCurdy & Rhodes
Builder	Arma Marine

Round the World
Jean Michel Viant
    (Skipper)
Bruno Caire
Gerard Caire
Luc Billard
Benedicte Lunven
Jean Bernard Leonardi

Legs 1, 2, 3
Thierry Lunven
Claude Letz
Thierry Norman

Legs 2, 3
Vincent Devictor

Legs 2, 3, 4
Jean Louis Sabarly

Legs 1, 2
Patrick Therond

Leg 1
Philippe Pelsmaeker
Serge Bosmorin

Leg 3
Frederic Pey
Philippe Bougoim

Leg 4
Anne Maria Sabatier
Serge Vayrette

Kings Legend

LOA	64 feet 6 inches
LWL	47 feet
Beam	16 feet 4 inches
Draft	9 feet 2 inches
Displacement	25.6 tons
Yacht club	Aldeburgh
First launched	1975
Designer	Sparkman & Stephens
Builder	Nautor

Round the World
John Roberts
Gregary Tuxworth
William Porter
Edward Allison
Hans Savimaki
James Novak

Legs 1, 3, 4
Nicholas Ratcliff
    (Skipper 1, 3, 4)

Legs 1, 2, 3
Michael Clancy
    (Skipper 2)
Charles McKee
W. D. Birchenough Jnr.

Legs 2, 3, 4
Byran Dawson

Leg 1
Jack Bossert

Leg 2
Richard Bertie

Leg 4
Jean Vincent Blondiou
Christopher Barker
Jacques Sarasin

167

Neptune

LOA	59 feet 5 inches
LWL	46 feet 5 inches
Beam	17 feet 6 inches
Draft	9 feet 1 inch
Displacement	21.1 tons
Yacht club	St Jacut de la Mer
First launched	1977
Designer	André Mauric
Builder	Pouvreau

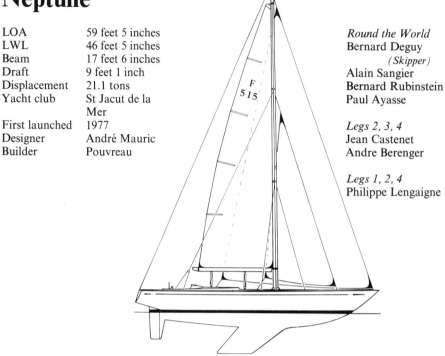

Round the World
Bernard Deguy
  (Skipper)
Alain Sangier
Bernard Rubinstein
Paul Ayasse

Legs 2, 3, 4
Jean Castenet
Andre Berenger

Legs 1, 2, 4
Philippe Lengaigne

Legs 1, 2
Dominique Lacroix
Daniel Gilles
Jean Marc Domange

Legs 3, 4
Jacques Hamelle
Bernard Donnezan

Leg 1
Gilles Vaton
Claude Rigal

Leg 3
Pascal Marty
Alain Caudrelier

Leg 4
Philippe Court

Tielsa

LOA	63 feet 4 inches
LWL	52 feet 8 inches
Beam	16 feet 3 inches
Draft	8 feet 9 inches
Displacement	27 tons
Yacht club	Ver van Uust Zeilers
First launched	1977
Designer	Johan Elsenga
Builder	Jachtbouw Noord Nederland

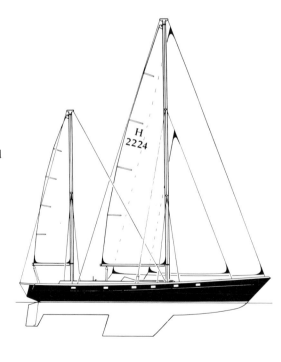

Round the World
Dirk Nauta
  (Skipper)
Mat Padmos
Sjerp Noorda
Robert Kwekkeboom
Ben de Ruyter
Ieke Dusseljee
Erick Ader
Bob Hanenberg
Ruedi Zimmermann
Anton Dusseljee
Arjan Schouten
Dirk Reidel

Leg 3
Jan Heogland

Traite de Rome

LOA	51 feet 2 inches
LWL	35 feet 1 inch
Beam	13 feet 1 inch
Draft	7 feet 8 inches
Displacement	13 tons
Yacht club	Sail for Europe
First launched	1975
Designer	Sparkman & Stephens
Builder	Huisman, Vollenhove

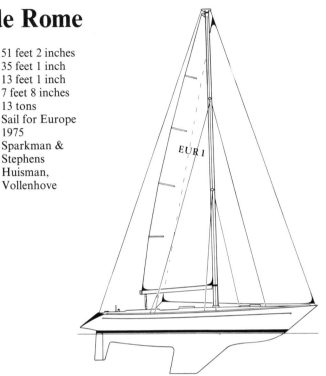

Round the World
Philippe Hanin
(Skipper)
Frederick Heinemann
Judith Herbert
Jan Rens
Antonio Chioatto
Stig Bovbjerg

Legs 2, 3, 4
Tomas Ruether

Legs 2, 3
Robert Giradin
Jean Blondiou

Leg 1
Philippe Soetaert
Patricia Colmant
Jean Marc Frantz

Leg 4
Jacques Pochon
Harold Cudmore

33 Export

LOA	56 feet 4 inches
LWL	42 feet 10 inches
Beam	13 feet 4 inches
Draft	8 feet 4 inches
Displacement	12 tons
Yacht club	Française de Sport
First launched	1968
Designer	André Mauric
Builder	Acnam

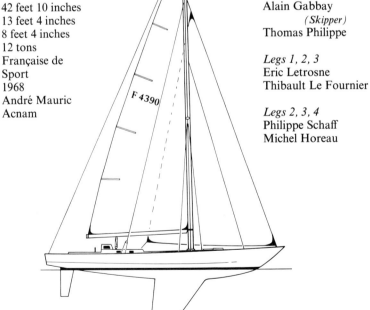

Round the World
Alain Gabbay
(Skipper)
Thomas Philippe

Legs 1, 2, 3
Eric Letrosne
Thibault Le Fournier

Legs 2, 3, 4
Philippe Schaff
Michel Horeau

Legs 2, 3
G. S. Parisis

Leg 1
Jean Louis Sabarly
Patrice Dumas
Yves Allemant
Paul Mothe

Leg 2
Sylvie Delinondes
Y. B. Foucou

Leg 4
Pascal Marty
Maxime Laloux
Vincent Devictor
Thierry Lunven

Appendix III Results and Prizes

AROUND THE WORLD RACE RESULTS—26,950 sea miles

	Yacht	Rating	Elapsed Time (Hours)	Corrected Time (Hours)	(Days)
1	*Flyer*	48.4	3269.48	2857.01	119
2	*Kings Legend*	48.4	3327.79	2915.29	121
3	*Traite de Rome*	35.7	3716.97	2922.85	122
4	*Disque D'Or*	46.2	3408.63	2938.94	122
5	*ADC Accutrac*	46.9	3495.47	3044.31	127
6	*Gauloises II*	38.1	3767.01	3055.91	127
7	*Adventure*	37.5	3806.21	3074.92	128
8	*Neptune*	44.3	3653.56	3131.88	130
9	*B & B Italia*	41.5	3773.58	3170.38	132
10	*33 Export*	39.7	3951.53	3192.52	133
11	*Tielsa*	50.0	3565.37	3192.60	133
12	*Great Britain II*	68.4	3228.38	3226.72	134
13	*Debenhams*	41.3	3869.09	3259.83	136
14	*Japy Hermes*	45.1	3937.49	3438.00	143
15	*Heath's Condor*	68.8	3433.70	3456.16	144

Leg Results

Leg 1   Portsmouth to Cape Town 6,650 sea miles

	Yacht	Elapsed Time (Hours)	Corrected Time (Hours)
1	*Flyer*	932.90	829.87
2	*Kings Legend*	934.90	831.87
3	*Gauloises II*	1035.31	858.59
4	*Disque D'Or*	991.75	874.61
5	*Traite de Rome*	1091.95	894.75
6	*Adventure*	1080.87	899.17
7	*B & B Italia*	1061.47	911.39
8	*Neptune*	1051.92	921.94
9	*ADC Accutrac*	1036.89	924.32
10	*Tielsa*	1030.00	936.75
11	*Debenhams*	1089.10	937.51
12	*Great Britain II*	965.60	963.95
13	*33 Export*	1206.21	1042.35
14	*Japy-Hermes*	1237.71	1113.21
15	*Heath's Condor*	1207.48	1224.90*

* Includes penalty

Leg 2   Cape Town to Auckland 7,400 sea miles

	Yacht	Elapsed Time (Hours)	Corrected Time (Hours)
1	*33 Export*	830.92	650.42
2	*Traite de Rome*	876.03	658.43
3	*Kings Legend*	771.84	659.03
4	*Flyer*	773.04	660.25
5	*Disque D'Or*	801.18	672.67
6	*Adventure*	875.65	675.30
7	*ADC Accutrac*	822.61	699.18
8	*Heath's Condor*	729.06	730.90
9	*Great Britain II*	750.57	750.57
10	*Neptune*	913.93	771.14
11	*Debenhams*	944.20	777.36
12	*B & B Italia*	944.19	779.05
13	*Japy-Hermes*	920.63	783.93
14	*Tielsa*	901.52	799.61
15	*Gauloises II*	1068.71	873.90

Leg 3   Auckland to Rio de Janeiro 7,400 sea miles

	Yacht	Elapsed Time (Hours)	Corrected Time (Hours)
1	*Gauloises II*	896.40	701.59
2	*Flyer*	821.39	708.58
3	*Traite de Rome*	951.23	733.64
4	*Disque D'Or*	880.37	751.86
5	*ADC Accutrac*	887.00	763.58
6	*Neptune*	907.09	764.30
7	*Kings Legend*	880.20	767.39
8	*Tielsa*	881.45	779.55
9	*B & B Italia*	945.75	780.58
10	*Great Britain II*	808.77	808.77*
11	*Heath's Condor*	809.17	811.01
12	*Debenhams*	987.29	820.45
13	*Japy-Hermes*	957.80	821.11***
14	*Adventure*	1027.59	827.24
15	*33 Export*	1037.08	856.58**

*   Includes 10 min penalty
**   Includes 5 min penalty
*** Includes 2 hour allowance for assisting
33 Export

Leg 4   Rio de Janeiro to Portsmouth 5,500 sea miles

	Yacht	Elapsed Time (Hours)	Corrected Time (Hours)
1	*Gauloises II*	766.60	621.82
2	*Traite de Rome*	797.75	636.03
3	*Disque D'Or*	735.33	639.81
4	*33 Export*	777.32	643.16
5	*Kings Legend*	740.85	657.00
6	*ADC Accutrac*	748.97	657.23
7	*Flyer*	742.14	658.30
8	*Adventure*	822.11	673.21
9	*Neptune*	780.62	674.49
10	*Tielsa*	752.42	676.69
11	*Heath's Condor*	687.99	679.22
12	*B & B Italia*	822.17	699.40
13	*Great Britain II*	703.43	703.43
14	*Japy-Hermes*	821.34	719.74
15	*Debenhams*	848.51	724.51

Around the World Prizes

Winner	**The Whitbread Trophy**	*Flyer*
Second	Royal Naval and Royal Albert Yacht Club Trophy	*Kings Legend*
Third	Royal Thames Yacht Club Velsheda Trophy	*Traite de Rome*
First on elapsed time	Portsmouth City Council Trophy R.N.S.A. Gold Dolphin	*Great Britain II* *Great Britain II*
Outstanding Seamanship	Lady Swaythling Trophy	*Japy-Hermes*
Yacht with best corrected time whose crew included a lady on each leg	Lady Mackworth Trophy	*Traite de Rome*
Best kept log	Trinity House Prize	*Flyer*
Winning team	Long John International Trophy and for each leg	*Flyer* *Kings Legend* *Disque D'Or*
Best position reporting	Nautor Trophy	*Tielsa*
Yacht maintained in best condition	*Flyer* Trophy	*Neptune*
Special award	Jacquet Trophy	*Traite de Rome*
Special award	R.N.S.A. (Vancouver Branch) Barrel of Rum	The Fleet
Each yacht to finish	R.N.S.A. Bronze Trophy	All yachts
Each crew member to finish	R.N.S.A. Plaques	All crews

Cape Town to Rio

First on handicap	Roaring Forties Trophy	*Flyer*

The Whitbread Trophy was designed by the famous silversmith Gerald Benney, holder of all three Royal Warrants. He stated that he intended to give an impression of the overpowering seas together with the smallness of the yachts racing.

1 Portsmouth to Cape Town

Winner	City of Cape Town Trophy	*Flyer*
Second	Cruising Association of South Africa Trophy	*Kings Legend*
Third	Royal Cape Town Yacht Club Trophy	*Gauloises II*
First on elapsed time	South African Wool Board Trophy R.N.S.A. Silver Dolphin	*Flyer*
Winning Team	Long John International Trophy	*Flyer* *Kings Legend* *Disque D'Or*
Best Log	Caleuche Prize	*Flyer*
Each yacht to finish	Cruising Association of South Africa Plaques	All yachts

2 Cape Town to Auckland

Winner	Royal New Zealand Yacht Squadron Trophy	*33 Export*
Second	Royal New Zealand Yacht Squadron Trophy	*Traite de Rome*
Third	Royal New Zealand Yacht Squadron Trophy	*Kings Legend*
First on elapsed time	R.N.S.A. Silver Dolphin	*Heath's Condor*
Winning Team	Long John International Trophy	*Flyer* *Kings Legend* *Disque D'Or*
Most outstanding passage	Brownson Jewellery Trophy	*Gauloises II*
First lady home	Girard Perragoux Trophy	Diana Thomas-Ellam *(Great Britain II)*
Best log	Caleuche Prize	*Adventure*

174

3   Auckland to Rio de Janeiro

Winner	Iate Clube do Rio de Janeiro Trophy	*Gauloises II*
Second	Iate Clube do Rio de Janeiro Trophy	*Flyer*
Third	Iate Clube do Rio de Janeiro Trophy	*Traite de Rome*
First on elapsed time	R.N.S.A. Silver Dolphin	*Great Britain II*
Winning Team	Long John International Trophy	*Flyer* *Kings Legend* *Disque D'Or*
Best log	Caleuche Prize	*Flyer*

4   Rio to Portsmouth

Winner	Royal Ocean Racing Club Trophy	*Gauloises II*
Second	Rod Rigging Trophy	*Traite de Rome*
Third	Lively Lady Trophy	*Disque D'Or*
First on elapsed time	R.N.S.A. Silver Dolphin Henri Lloyd Trophy	*Heath's Condor* *Heath's Condor*
Winning Team	Long John International Trophy	*Flyer* *Kings Legend* *Disque D'Or*
Best log	Caleuche Prize	*Flyer*

175